# Lessons Mama Never Taught Me

## What Every Woman Should Know

Dr. Karen R. January

# Forward

The purpose of this book was to share actual real life stories with other women, mothers and future mothers in hopes of strengthening, improving, and encouraging an open and honest dialogue between a mother and her daughter(s). The women who contributed to this writing felt strongly about sharing their personal experiences while growing up with their mothers. Their conversations are intimate and focus primarily on the lessons, topics, and questions that were avoided and how the lack of communication impacted and affected their lives.

They consented to participate in this endeavor as a freeing and healing opportunity for women who may have encountered some of the same or similar experiences. It was a cathartic release for them and a means to hopefully encourage other women to face their own past and present struggles. They wanted to speak on how they were able to deal with their challenges (*mentally, emotionally, spiritually, and physically)*, the lessons they learned... and the paths they chose toward healing. They concluded that it is not always easy to move forward from life's challenges but we do have the strength to try. We just have to continue to dig deep inside.

The life experiences that are addressed are all issues that are relevant today. Self- esteem, teen pregnancy, drug abuse, domestic violence, dating, sexual assault, cheating, racism, mental illness, bullying, body image, obesity and relationships are some of the topics explored. Not only is it important for mothers to address these current social issues with their daughters but it is crucial that fathers discuss them with their sons as well.

*Please be advised that the following stories contain graphic language and explicit adult material.

# Acknowledgements

I would like to thank everyone for their valuable time, guidance and sincere interest in this project. I extend my heartfelt gratitude to you.

To my sons Jarret and Corey Mays, your many accomplishments and determination to succeed continue to inspire me. You have taught me that there are no limitations in what you can achieve. Thank you for encouraging me to live my dreams.

To my cousin Laverne, you have been my strength and motivation throughout this entire journey. You are always there for me.

To my mother O.J., I appreciate your endless years of support you have given me and the things you did teach me.

To my Literary team Dr. Reginald Hardaway and Soror Deborah Matthews your support and dedication never waivered and for that I truly appreciate you.

A special thanks to all of the women who gave of their time to share their personal stories candidly without any reservations. If it were not for you this book would not have been possible.

Amen...

# Table of Contents

**Let's Meet the Women**

# Introduction

Think back for a moment... Do you remember how you learned about sex, drugs, boys, and life in general? This question was posed to women from the baby boomers age, and the "X" and "Y" generations. The number one response was they learned most of their information from their *"girlfriends"*. The number two response was "the media." Now, don't get me wrong, some did learn about sex, drugs, boys, and other things from their mothers or other significant family members. Overall, it seems that there are current relevant topics (sex, teen pregnancy, drugs, relationships to name a few that some mothers have failed to address with their daughters.

Talking to our daughters about sensitive issues can be an ordeal that is dreaded by many moms. Is it that mothers are too embarrassed to speak on these subjects? Are they uninformed? Or, maybe they just don't know what to say or how to say it. Some mothers touch on it where others would rather avoid the entire matter altogether. The remaining mothers have resigned to allowing their daughters to figure out life on their own. Whether mothers want to talk about it or not, it needs to be said. *"The Talk"* between a mother and daughter is a rites of passage ceremony that will allow our young women to travel with some degree of confidence and knowledge through the matrix of life.

As women, it is our responsibility to ensure that our children are properly prepared with the life skills they will need for day-to-day living in this society. We must address their social emotional, spiritual, physical, and financial well-being. Bullying, dating, violence, and sexting are some of the social ills that are consuming our youth, schools and communities. These concerns are proof that we as a society must intervene by providing open discussions, preventive measures and resources for support so "our daughters" will become positive, contributing productive citizens and future parents. The bond between mothers and daughters can and should be a stepping-stone and turning point in building and shaping relationships that will have a lasting impact on their life experiences and relationships.

In many kitchens across the globe, mothers may have witnessed their young children trying to touch the fire on the stove. We were immediately told that the fire was hot and if we touched it we were going to get burned. It would be a good bet that quite a few of us at some point touched the fire on the stove anyway. We did not heed the warning and we got burned.

It doesn't matter how many times someone tells us how deep the water is, we may feel that person doesn't know what they are talking about and we then make a conscious decision not to listen. Sometimes, we just have to find out the hard way and personally discover that *"Fat meat really is greasy."* It is a monumental victory if we can learn from others' mistakes without having to test the actual waters ourselves. Unfortunately things do not always work out that way.

I want to make this very clear. This book was not intended to discredit or condemn the mothers who made monumental sacrifices, worked effortlessly and served the role of both mother and father to their daughter and/or sons. Motherhood is one job that cannot be perfected. It's one of the most challenging and toughest jobs in the world.

The voices of these women came from all walks of life, ethnic backgrounds, varied religious practices and age groups. The stories are from actual life experiences and events and one of the narratives told is mine. Names have been changed to protect their identities. If you should recognize a character or narrative that is familiar, it is only coincidental.

# Prologue

Many of us have memories of growing up. Some were good and others we would like to forget about all together. In some households there were certain phrases mothers would say to us that were considered *"teachable moments."* As I think back, I didn't understand as a child what any of those phrases meant. They made absolutely no sense at all for example: "What you do in the dark, will come out in the light". "If you lie down with dogs, you'll get up with fleas". "You made your bed, now lie in it." And, "What did I tell you?" I had to back track and refresh my memory bank to remember exactly what it was that she had actually said.

Some of her expressions weren't verbalized. They were never spoken but it was certainly understood. They were understood and known as the *"look."* In case you don't know what the look is, it was *"eye contact"* with a facial gesture to let you know that you had crossed the line. The look meant that discipline would be administered if your behavior didn't improve quickly. You knew immediately, if you didn't stop whatever you were doing, (*and it didn't matter if you were in a grocery store or church*) there would be consequences to pay when you got home. Nine times out of ten it worked. You didn't want that beat down in private or public. If you attempted to defy your mom and continue the behavior you were escorted briskly sometimes by your ear to the nearest washroom to suffer the consequences.

I remember *"the look"* on one occasion when I asked her if I could get pregnant from kissing a boy. This was one of the primary conversations of discussions that my female classmates and

I would laugh and giggle about during recess. My mom's face and her *"look"* informed me that I should not have asked that question. Her response was "You don't talk about things like that. Nice girls don't talk about or do things like that." My next question was well, "What is it that nice girls don't do?" I got the mama look again. I waited and waited for my mom's explanation... eleven years old... twelve years old... and thirteen years old... but my question was never answered. I never bothered to ask her anything else again. I figured I would not get an answer, just the mama look. We never talked on that subject again.

Couldn't Mama see I was growing up? I needed guidance to make those important day-to-day decisions that would affect and shape my unpredictable world. I needed more than just a list of do's and don'ts. I needed her to speak the unspoken words and get past the topics that were considered taboo to her. I needed her to quench my thirst and answer the many questions that were mysteries to me. We never talked about puberty, self-esteem, self-image, or the dreaded *"period."* Sure, she provided me with books to read but somehow the messages intended were lost. I had the manual but no one explained to me what peg went into what hole. You can have all the pieces to a puzzle and still not be able to put it together. Sometimes, you need a little help.

Young girls in the 70's and even today huddle together snickering and whispering to exchange and share information on numerous subjects. They have not tested them to determine if they are fact or fiction. In their minds it doesn't matter if the information is fact or fiction. *"The girls"* are just a source of comfort and support to each other to validate the myths of growing up that they have made their own reality.

All I wanted was some insight or wisdom to understand the changes I was experiencing physically and mentally. Adolescence can be complicated and complex. There are many factors affecting the emotional, psychological, social emotional and cultural development during the pre-teen years. Drugs, gangs, pregnancy, peer pressure, and racism are just some of the vital issues that parents should explain and discuss with their children and how these social conditions can have a lasting impact on their lives. I, like many of my peers at that time, needed to know what becoming a woman was about and what experiences I would face in the process.

My mom could have told me, "Men should always treat you with gentleness and respect. You should never tolerate or accept anything less even if it means being without a man." Unfortunately, I had to learn this the hard way from too many broken hearts and crushed self-esteem. Eventually, I did finally get the message that I had to love myself more than loving a man.

I remember when we went to visit my mom's best friend in California. When we arrived at her home my mom and her friend could not wait to escape into the kitchen to catch up on all the latest news. I guess they forgot about me. They left me in the living room with her husband Mr. Gaines. He was more than hospitable to entertain me in their absence. He welcomed me to come and sit on his lap and not knowing any better I did. Mr. Gaines seemed to be having a good time rocking me back and forth. He was bouncing me up and down on his lap like a baby. In actuality, I really was. As I look back now I realize that he was getting his jollies on. He was having dry sex with a nine year old. I was so scared because no man had ever done this to me before. What was I supposed to do? What was I supposed to say? I decided not to say or do anything because I didn't want to get into any trouble. It's funny though, even as a child you usually have a second sense when something is wrong.

It wasn't long before my turbulent ride was over and just in time. My mother and Mrs. Gaines returned to the living room just as I was getting off Mr. Gaines's lap. It was interesting that they both looked at me strangely and asked if everything was all right. It was as if they too had sensed something was going on. I told them I was fine. In later years when I was older and exposed to the ins and outs of sex I realized that Mr. Gaines's real name was Mr. Pedophile.

There were so many things and lessons that I wish my mom had shared with me for example, "boys" and even grown men are going to ask you to do things not in your best interest. They may ask you to do things that you don't want to do like touching your body or their body parts inappropriately." Mom should have told me that, it was perfectly okay to say "No"!" mean it and stand by it. Or, when in doubt, tell an adult if needed to ask for help.

Most importantly, I needed to know the truth about being a girl of color in North America and of the world. I needed to know that my kinky hair, chocolate skin, round behind and wide hips were a blessing... and not a curse. I didn't have to fit in or meet society's standards for beauty (*a size 2, with long straight hair, thin lips and a Roman shaped nose*). I was already beautiful just the way I was!

As I got older I found that I was always being compared to some other mother's child. This didn't help my self-esteem at all. I remember my mom saying, "Why can't you be more like Jessica? (*she was my best friend*). She's so smart. She's on the honor roll. She is going to be admitted to a top high school. She's at the top of her class and she's not fast like you!" Instead of always comparing me to Jessica, I wished she had acknowledged some of my accomplishments and guided me more toward becoming a young lady. I should have been told that I was intelligent, confident, and that I was capable of achieving my life goals. I didn't have to be like Jessica. I could just be me and that was good enough.

I needed to know that after my parents divorced and we moved away, my father would not be there to defend me and that I would no longer be able to look to him or depend on him to find solace and protection. I didn't know that my father would just disappear from my life just like the child support payments that were supposed to come. I have often wondered if my mother had prepared me for some of the bumps in the road that I have experienced would my life have turned out differently. No one can answer that but at least maybe I could have had a running start.

My story, as well as some of yours is very relevant to what many other young girls' stories are and what they are faced with today. Even as adults we still struggle with life's challenges. It is not about the color of our skin, culture, ethnic background, religious beliefs, or how smart we are. It is all about the commonalities we share, the journey that each of us has or will travel and the tools that are necessary for us to navigate successfully in our global society.

# one

# How my mother became my pimp

"Puppy love, teen idols, high school, pajama parties, hanging out at the mall, soccer practices and
games are things a twelve year old child should
be thinking about. Instead, my young innocence
was stripped away and my weekends were spent
"Kissing and licking it" and I don't mean ice cream!

*Melissa Harrington, 32 years old, Dallas, Texas*

There were good times and bad times growing up in Chicago. In
my household there were eight children, an unemployed mother
(*Daddy wanted mom to stay home with the kids*) and a father who
was employed as a factory worker making a little over minimum
wage. In our family there were certainly more bad times than good.
Trying to feed and clothe all of us was not an easy task. Even though
money was tight, there was plenty of love to go around. I soon
found out that love is not all it's made out to be. I never understood
what my parents saw in each other. They were complete opposites.
Daddy was a quiet and mild mannered man and mama was a party
girl. She liked to listen to her music and dance while she was sip-
ping on her cheap wine poured into her cracked coffee mug. Little
did I know that my stay at home mom was always busy with other

1

interests. I discovered that while daddy was away at work, mom was at play. I don't know how she did it with eight children but she seemed to find a way. Maybe having an outside lover was her release from the all the pressures of raising a family. Mama still wanted to have a good time even though she was married. She was stuck at home all the time with us and I guess this was her outlet. It was definitely an out for my Dad. He must have found out something because one day he got up to leave for work and that was the last time we saw him.

Mama tried to explain why daddy left us. She said it was a difficult task for anybody to provide for a large family with little or nothing. I thought that maybe it was my little sister's fault. She had leukemia and her medical bills were so high that it might have been too much for daddy to handle in addition to everything else. Personally, I think it was mama who drove him away while sowing her wild seeds and daddy wasn't going for that. Whatever the reason was he never came back and he didn't leave a forwarding address.

It's hard enough as it is to make a living with two parents working let alone one parent working and getting by with near or below minimum wages and lack of insurance benefits. When a family is torn apart and a wife and children are left to fend for themselves, what are they to do? Parents can only provide what they are capable of doing. Families can only attempt to survive in the situation and circumstances that they have been given and try to make the best of it.

It's easy for some people to relax in their personal comfort zones and criticize the *"have nots,"* while they sit back in their leather chairs watching television programs on their 50" flat screen T.V's, driving their gas guzzling SUV's and dining in the finest restaurants with linen covered tablecloths and drinking water from crystal glasses. That is the American dream that is shared by many. Others find themselves in a less fortunate situation due to their placement or station in life which is nobody's fault.

You would think the massive taxes that the middle class and poor people pay would afford them a few more pieces of the pie and benefits that some citizens seem to get more of. What about the middle class and poor people's share? After all, we are the laborers that make this country work. Sitting on one's ass passing gas instead of passing laws that do not benefit the masses is an insult and injustice to the working class.

After daddy left our family was torn apart and we were left to survive the best way we could. We were on the brink of homelessness and one meal away from starvation. My mother could barely read or write and her job skills were lacking. With eight children including my sick sister, she needed to be at home. Without our father as a caretaker and no support system in place, we were about to go down without a life vest. Just the thought of being without the basic necessities like food, clothing and a roof over our heads sent me into a world that was unthinkable for a thirteen year old child. My mother was desperate and our world was about to cave in. To this day I still can't believe the solution my mother proposed to save our family. It was shameful and horrendous but she convinced me that if we were going to survive it was the only way. I was not about to get a lesson in morals, values, self-respect, integrity or what dignity was all about.

The only knowledge that I had on the subject of sex was what I read about or saw on television and of course, Carter Jacobs. We had fooled around experimenting with each other's body parts. Most kids our age probably did the same thing. You may have even done so. I found out the real deal when I started selling my body to save my family from a life of poverty and despair. In exchange I was the one who began living a life of despair. There would be no more sweet dreams for this innocent child. I quickly became a slave to grown men for their personal pleasures. I characterized the trade off as a means to an end. The men got what they wanted and my family had food, clothing, a place to stay, and most importantly my sickly sister was getting the medical attention she needed. It is said, "... On this earth we all have our crosses to bear." Well, this one was mine. Mama said, "There was no other way."

If you are judging me, then I'm glad you grew up in a world where decisions like the one that was made for me was unthinkable. On the other hand it is possible you may not be as sensitized to how the rest of the world lives. You think this was our choice? At that time it was the only option on the table. I know you're thinking, "Why didn't my mama sell her vagina?" You can answer that question yourself. You know that men like those fresh young tight bodies...sweet meat... not a body of a worn out mother of eight.

Whether your eyes are open or not, you should look at what's really going on around you. Maybe you don't know what it's like to be poor, hungry or where you will lay your head each night. I know my mom was supposed to accept her responsibility and protect her children with her very own life. Even the animal kingdom does that. It's very easy to talk about morals and values when your rent is paid and your hierarchy of needs has been met. The saying "Until you've walked in my shoes..." is quite relevant. You never know what life will bring you or what you might have to do to survive.

Morals and values first begin in the home. We send our children to school as another means to learn morals from other people's experiences. We wind up either copying behaviors negative or positive or we develop our own. Were the choices made in my life a moral issue, a survival issue or both? Where was the right to my free will, to be left alone and unmolested? In my case morality was determined by a desperate conscious mind concluding that morals were for sale.

Cody, an older cousin of mine, was the go between to set up my sexual escapades. He used his run down studio apartment as the sex den for me to meet my predators. From what I could guess, the men ranged from the ages of 25-45 years old. I would get paid from $100 to $300 dollars per male depending on Cody's negotiations. I never saw a dime. It went straight to my mom to care for our family and medical assistance for my sister and the rest went to Cody. The plan was that I attend school during the week and work on weekends. The money was always paid up front before show time. That way there was no haggling about the money after their sperm had been deposited inside of me or in a condom.

I would service about four to six men on Friday and Saturday nights. The predators were scheduled between 5 p.m. and sometimes up until 1a.m. I would bring in about $900.00 a night depending on how many hounds showed up. They certainly loved pawing over this young tender flesh. In a perfect world sex should be a warm loving caring experience with a man that you care about and vice versa. That would not be the case for me.

I was instructed by Cody to give the predators a condom. I had heard of condoms but I didn't know anything about how they were supposed to be used. He told me to watch and make sure they put it on. I did but I'm not sure they always used it on the second go round. I'm not even sure they used it the first go round.

The first time I hear is always the hardest and that was no lie. I was nervous with my first predator. As he came towards me I could smell the alcohol and weed on his breath. I knew it was weed because I had smelled it on Cody many times before. He was rough and much too big for my fragile 5 foot 5 inch height and 98 pound body frame. I endured as best I could as he groped and sweated all over me. After he left I cried like the baby I really was laying there in a pool of blood. I concluded that I was no longer a virgin.

I assumed that these men had no conscious because they had no problem pumping up and down on this child. Hell where was my mother's and Cody's conscious? Some would say that I should have told someone like my school counselor. I couldn't do that. If I did my family would be split up and it would never be the same again. I loved my brothers and sisters and I didn't want us to be apart. Anyway, it was too late. The ball was rolling and there was no turning back now.

Most of the men I encountered had little or no conversation. After all, what conversation could a grown male have with a thirteen-year old child? They were all just a bunch of perverts. There was one in particular who did want to talk. He looked young and worked as a janitor at a school. I felt sorry for those young girls at his school. I wondered if he was looking at them the way he was looking at me. I wondered if he had ever coaxed one of them into the bathroom and had a conversation with them. Vince mostly talked about his childhood and how his father would wait for his mother to go to work. She worked the night shift. When she left for work, he said, "My father would slither into my bedroom like a snake and force me to have sex with him." He said my father told me "If you ever say anything to anyone, especially your mother, I would make sure you never see her again." Vince said he was only nine years old when this happened to him.

Vince continued to return to me many more nights than I wished. I knew he was suffering in silence like I was. Every time he would come to see me he would just keep saying over and over, "I'm sorry. I'm so sorry. Please don't be mad at me." I cried every time he touched me. I was probably feeling the same pain he was. Fortunately, for him his mom got sick at work one day and came home. You know what she found when she got there. She found her husband in bed with her son. He said, "At that moment I felt my prayers were finally answered and this nightmare was now over." On the flip side my nightmare was still going on and there was no sign when I would be saved. All I did was lie there and wonder who would be next. It didn't matter because there would be another predator right after him. Weekend after weekend they kept coming, the old ones and the new ones.

There was another sicko who seemed to enjoy pain. Boy, was I getting an education but no diploma to show for it. He would bring a little black bag with him. I called it "the bag of tricks." There were all kinds of weird things in there. He had whips, belts, vibrators, leather gloves, ropes, handcuffs, wigs, and the most bizarre thing was a police costume that he made me wear. Help! I think it was right here that I was really scarred for my life. I was terrified because I didn't understand what these props were all about. It made no sense to me. Why would it? Tying a grown man up, smacking him with whips, and sticking a vibrating dick in his ass were both terrifying In the back of my mind I was fearful that he would use his vibrator on me and Lord knows where he might stick it. It was funny because I had never seen a grown man ask to be spanked with a belt or punished and then thanking me for doing it. The thought of being hand cuffed, tied up and slapped with leather gloves on my ass was not my idea of a good time. He would always say that he was a bad boy and needed to be punished. I have no idea what he was being punished for. He never told me and I never asked. I do know that Cody always charged him more for his theatrical antics.

As I think back, some things I just wasn't mentally or emotionally able to handle. Oral sex was one. That's what one predator liked for me to do to him. He would always tell me to "kiss it." I had no clue what he was talking about but he was quick to show me what I needed to do. I gagged and choked until I threw up. Vomit was everywhere and all over him. The predator was so angry he started slapping me in my face. Cody heard my screams and came into the room to see what was going on. He told him "Get out and don't come back again." Cody could see that I was in no shape or condition to work the rest of the night. He told me to get cleaned up and then he took me home. It's funny how things change because after that incident as the weeks and months went by I did learn how to *"kiss it."*

By the time I was fourteen, I had become quite a pro and knew most of the tricks of the trade (*I guess that was a pun*). By this time my family was surviving and my sister was getting the medical care that she needed. My mother continued to stay at home and raise the kids but no one was raising me. I often wondered did she ever feel any guilt or remorse for what she had done. I believe she actually convinced herself that it was for the good of keeping the family together. I tried to tell her that I was psychologically, emotionally, and mentally drained and I didn't know how much more of this I could take. In her mind all she could vision is that we weren't homeless. All I could think about was how much I loved my sister and that she was medically being cared for.

I thought I had seen it all, but Francine, yes, Francine was a woman. I wondered why Francine wasn't with a man. She was so pretty and she could have had any man she wanted with a snap of her fingers. For some reason she needed...wanted to be with a woman. she too, brought a bag of tricks with her. Her bag was much different though. She pulled out what looked like a belt and I thought for a minute she was going to beat me. Then, I looked a little closer and to my surprise it had a penis attached to it. I wondered, "What the hell was this?" She began strapping it to the lower part of her body and the rest is history. About now, I think I have seen and heard it all. Basically, my sexual identity was fucked up, literally. I was almost certain I would experience role confusion at some point in my life and that I would be mentally unbalanced forever. What I experienced at such a young age made me grow up faster than I should have and it turned me into a promiscuous out of control teen. Things would soon take a turn that would change everybody's life forever including cousin Cody's. My living hell was about to change.

A couple of years later, predator Bill entered the picture. He was a 28 year-old handsome man. He was finer than wine and good as gold. I say *"He was good as gold"* because he was a teenager's dream financially. He was the only predator that didn't treat me like shit.

He treated me like a woman. He made me feel special. Bill would talk to me like I was a grown up and not like a child. Even though, in the eyes of the law I was a child and jail bait at that.

Bill became my savior, my all. He rescued me like a knight in shining armor and helped me to release some of my psychological, mental, and emotional bondage that I was trapped in. I was a fifteen year-old girl about to be sixteen and we can be quite impressionable when someone is giving them little trinkets and filling their heads with the kind of bull that makes you blush and giggle. It didn't take much for me to be happy. Getting my nails done, hair done, buying designer jeans, gym shoes, and purses were the *"things"* that Bill filled my little pathetic and empty world with. Even though those *"things"* were only material, they were a big comfort to me.

As bizarre as this may sound, I started having feelings for this man. No, it wasn't a crush. To me it was love. So, what does a fifteen-year old talk about with a 28-year-old man? Now, remember, I had grown up fast. I became mature quickly beyond my years. We talked about everything from music, to places we wanted to see, and about his job. He was a district sales manager for a well-known department store. I can say there is one in just about every major city. He would tell me about his day at work and I would talk about my family. Strange though, he never talked about his family, and I never asked. I didn't care I just wanted to be loved. Later, it would be crystal clear why he didn't. Sometimes, we would just talk about life and things we wanted to do. I told him I wanted to be a doctor and he always encouraged me. He said, "You can do anything you put your mind to" and I believed him.

Bill made me feel more than just a sex object. On his off days he would pick me up from school in his steel grey mustang convertible. We would go get something to eat or go to the movies. When he made love to me, he was gentle, caring and not pawing at me like a piece of meat the way the other predators did. He wasn't happy at all with my sexual encounters and how I was living my life. Bill wanted me all to himself but unless he could keep food on our table and pay the bills especially my sister's medical bills that wasn't going to happen.

Several weeks later, I found out why Bill never talked about his family. One weekend he came over for his scheduled weekly visit. We were engaged in a hot steamy embrace when all of sudden we heard "Where is he? I know he's here!" There were all kinds of curse words being yelled in the front room and furniture was crashing to the floor. It sounded like a fight was occurring.

Cody was yelling at the visitor. I heard a woman's voice screaming and demanding to know where her husband was. It seemed Bill's wife had followed him this particular night and watched him enter the apartment. I guess Cody thought it was an early predator and he opened the door. What an idiot? He never scheduled that closely together. So, he opened the door and let the hurricane in. Cody could not hold her back. She made her way into the bedroom where she found her husband and me ass naked. She went crazy for real. She started beating on Bill like a drum. I was terrified that I would be next. Fortunately, Bill and Cody were able to restrain her. That didn't last long. She broke loose and came after me. Adrenaline is powerful. She grabbed me and looked into my eyes and said, "You're just a child." When she said that, reality set in and she was right. I was no match or competition for her husband. I was a child and I had been fooling myself. I was just a little plaything to him with no future in it for me.

There's an old saying, "*The shit done hit the fan.*" and it did, lots of it. The first thing wifey did was call the police. In the meantime Bill was putting his clothes on and trying to explain what was going on. She wasn't hearing it. Why do men always say, "*This isn't what you think, she doesn't mean anything to me.*" When I heard him my heart must have broken into a thousand pieces and somehow I wanted to hurt him like he had just hurt me. So, I told wifey "It must have meant something because you were here every week like clock-work and you certainly didn't have to pick me up from school or buy me nice things." I got just the reaction I wanted. The "Mrs." started beating on him again and screaming, "I want you out of my house!" Meanwhile Cody was trying to hide receipts from all the predator transactions and clean up from the hurricane wifey brought before the police came. When they arrived she explained to them what was going on. She told them that both Bill and Cody were contributing to the delinquency of a minor. Immediately, Bill and Cody were arrested. Soon after a call was made to DCFS and I was turned over to them along with my brothers and sisters. We were all placed in foster care. Of course, no one was interested in taking on eight kids so we were split up for some time. What about Mom? She was arrested too and did time for negligence in the welfare of a minor and endangerment. The judge was hardest on her and Cody. Bill got time too and his wife divorced him. The other predators all went to jail too. Cody turned states' evidence to lessen his time. He turned everybody in since he had all the records (*names, addresses, telephone numbers, place of employment and paid receipts*).

Once Mom served her time, she was allowed to enter a parenting program in conjunction with her probation. She had to petition to do this through the courts if she wanted to try and get her kids back. The stipulations were that she must be gainfully employed and provide housing for us (*Which is what she should have done in the first place!*).

There were only three kids who went back with my mom. The remaining siblings were eighteen years of age and older. The older siblings had grown up in foster care without her. We had all moved on with our lives the best we could. I definitely could not find it in my heart to face her again. She had robbed me of the opportunity to be a child and fucked up my emotional and mental state of being. Maybe in time I will forgive her but right now it is still too painful. When Cody was released, he tried to contact me. What gall? I wasn't interested in anything he had to say. The both of them could suffer in hell like I did. What happened to me? I did go on to college and then was accepted into medical school. I became a Doctor of Internal Medicine and I am still a practicing physician.

The real twist and irony is this. I'm now a doctor seeing a doctor because one of my predators must have been infected with HIV and now, *SO AM I!* The moral of the story...it doesn't matter if you have one sexual partner or multiple sexual partners, the fluid is deadly when you engage in unprotected sex. **Stay protected!**

### What's The Lesson?

Teaching our daughters' morals, values, and integrity will affect how they view themselves and the world they live in. We want our daughters to develop and practice positive acceptable social behaviors so that their morals, principles, values, and self-esteem are not compromised.

Here are some steps that can be taken to instill and encourage moral development. Define the importance of integrity, dignity, and respect for self, kindness and compassion and then demonstrate these concepts on a daily basis. Have discussions with them on how they can demonstrate these behaviors too.

> ➢ Create hypothetical situations that will allow them to engage/learn how to get in touch with their emotions/feelings to establish a sense of right and wrong. Allow them to determine the course of action and the outcome of a responsible choice. An example may be "When one takes (*steals*) a toy from a store without paying for it, what are the consequences for this action?"
> ➢ Explain that there are consequences for inappropriate or unacceptable behaviors/choices. Look beyond the decision(s) made so they can see what action might possibly take place for that specific behavior. Explain if caught being

dishonest, it can make others doubt or stop believing in you, your actions or what you are saying.

➤ Modeling appropriate and positive behaviors are best. Offer yourself as an example to follow when it comes to morality issues. There must be some resemblance of morality in order to teach it! The devil will always go after the easiest pickings or weak-minded individuals.

**Be that, what you want your daughters to be!**

*two*

# The Maniac Husband from Cyberspace

"I was a single parent looking for love. I found it
(*of all places*) on the internet." They say, "Love is
blind." It must be because I couldn't see the forest for the trees. Once I said, "I do," the blindfold
soon came off and I was introduced to Dr. Jekyll
and Mr. Hyde. I watched the man I loved
become the raving maniac from cyberspace.

*Lisa Reed, 36 years, old Ann Arbor, Michigan*

I got tired of spending the weekends home alone playing computer
solitaire in my pajamas and late that night I decided to do something about it. I started looking for love on the Internet and after
hours of research I finally signed up with several popular computer
dating websites. I started looking right away. The men and choices
were plentiful and I met some really great guys. I always had "a
pair" and "a spare" to date. I had a lot of fun but there was no real
love connection with any of them.

Several months later that all changed and I began to chat online
with a man named Jeff. We communicated online and eventually on
the phone and via e-mail. We had several stimulating conversations

14

that would lead to us finally meeting in person. Our first date was a month later after our initial telephone conversation. I didn't want to rush things. I must admit I was little nervous about meeting someone that I didn't know anything about except what he had told me. We decided that we would meet at a restaurant in the downtown area. I was quite impressed with our meeting and especially how tall and handsome he was. We talked and took time to determine if there was a spark of interest between us. We even went for a nice long walk along the lake but from his conversation I wasn't sure if he was really interested in me. Maybe he didn't want to seem too excited. You know how some men are they want to be cool. When it was time to go he escorted me to my car and he asked me out for a second date and before he closed my door we shared quite a passionate kiss. After that, it was on. The relationship took off like a rocket into outer space. We were in our own world. To me, that was really good. Those boring weekend nights of solitaire in my pajamas were now a thing of the past.

We had a whirlwind courtship (*He was moving pretty fast and I didn't mind at it all*). But, that should have been a wake up call. HELLO! After our second date, we were inseparable and saw each other just about every day. I loved his consistency (*he always called when he said he would*), persistence, attention, his mind and his excitement about us. I felt so relaxed and safe around him. I didn't have to overlook his actions or anything he said, nor did I have to make things "*fit*"...we just did.

It was all- natural. I didn't have to hold my breath wondering what was next to come. In the past I was always looking for the other shoe to drop in the beginning stages of a relationship. The ones I had come in contact would talk too much, drink too much, were unbelievably cheap, had questionable stories about their lives, unemployed or under-employed, no car, in between jobs, living at home with mama, no communication skills, physically out of shape,... and the list goes on and on. You've probably been there and met those same kinds of men too. And you know what the funny part of this is? They always want a woman who is attractive and built like a brick shit house. They're not bringing anything to the table but they want you to bring the tablecloth, napkins, silverware, drinks, entre, and dessert. Oh, and let's not forget (*for you ladies who have been internet fishing*) when you meet them in person most times they don't look anything like their picture. They are good for posting pictures on the site when they were in high school when they didn't have the bald head and big stomach. Jeff didn't fit into any of the usual categories of my *un-datable* men. I was smitten by his charms and the way he treated me... like a queen.

I guess love is really blind because I couldn't see the forest for the trees. I didn't want to be apart from him. After only 3 months of dating I allowed him to start staying overnight at my house. He lived about fifty miles from where I lived so of course I didn't want him driving home alone late at night (*as if he couldn't*). Before I knew it, he had given up his apartment and moved in with me. Now, this might have been okay under any other circumstance but this was a *"no-no"* with me. I wanted to and needed to set a good example for my three daughters. I had never entertained the thought of a man being in my house with my girls but he was different. This is sometimes our downfall. We will make sacrifices to have a man in our lives.

I felt safe with Jeff. He was *"home"* to me. He was perfect in my eyes and could do no wrong. He was affectionate, adventurous, a world traveler, a professional educator, and most important of all he loved his mother. I've s always said, *"Any man that loves and takes care of his mother, is the man you want and he was good to her."* I don't know who said it but "That was a lie! "What was I thinking to let some Internet stranger move into my house with my three girls and me.

I tried to cover all the bases to get information about his background. This is very important to do if you're going to be in a relationship with someone. I asked him questions about his ex-wife and other questions about his past and former relationships. He would answer everything with no problem. He said that he had been married briefly for six months and had a son. He painted a picture of his ex wife as a woman who was easy to fly off the handle, difficult to get along with and wouldn't cooperate with him to allow visitation rights with his son. He portrayed himself as the victim of a bad marriage. It all seemed kind of one sided. He was so convincing that I willingly believed him. Remember, when a man blames a woman for everything and he didn't do anything wrong, fireworks should go off. Flags should be waving in the air. Volcanoes should be erupting in your mind. This was a sure sign of his unwillingness to tell me what part he played in the break up of the marriage.

She did allow him to visit his son on one occasion. He asked me to go with him so I had an opportunity to meet her. This was a few months before we were to be married. When I met her, I had an altogether different impression of who she was. She was actually someone who could have easily been a friend of mine. She was attractive, intelligent, personable and a doting mother. I didn't witness or feel any of this rage and irrational behavior he had expressed. In hindsight I should have paid more attention to what he said about her and realized it wasn't her it was more about him. It's funny how little clues and pieces of the puzzle are handed to you on a silver platter with champagne and you still don't pay any attention.

One of my cousins was enrolled at a University and was taking a course in psychology. At the time she didn't know that she was about to get a shocking surprise. One day she wore a university football shirt to class and that started a conversation with the professor because it happened to be one of his favorite teams. They started talking about the team and how it was doing. He was quite impressed that she knew so much about football. When he got home, he happened to mention the conversation to me. I asked him "What was the student's name?" He said, "Sherry." I yelled, "That's my cousin!" When I told her that Jeff was the guy I was dating, she couldn't believe how small the world is and that she would by chance just happen to be in his class. She informed me prior to you and Jeff getting together, that he was pretty tough and rough on the students. He was quite insensitive and very cocky. She said, "After you started dating him, his whole attitude changed. He was smiling now and seemed to be very happy and in love. Most of the students noticed the change and couldn't figure out why he was so much more personable but secretly I knew why.

One night before class started, Sherry called me and said, "I overheard some students discussing how they had taken a class with Jeff before." It appeared Jeff's wife had entered his class pretty upset one night and left several suitcases at the door. It seemed to be public knowledge, Sherri said, the other students were in agreement that this had taken place. That's when I should have started collecting clues and pieces to the puzzle of who this man really was. I never questioned him about this information since it was just hearsay. I always believed the old adage, *"Believe only half of what you see and none of what you hear."* I just swept it under the rug and left it there.

We were formally engaged one year after we met and married several months later. Only three days after we were married, Mr. Jekyl mysteriously disappeared and the evil Mr. Hyde appeared. Right away we had a big disagreement over my checking account. He wanted me to cash his check at my bank. I explained to him "My bank has a strict policy about cashing third party checks. They will not cash them." He told me "I was a liar." I called the bank to have them verify its check cashing policy as proof after which he told me "You only did that to make me look bad and make a fool out of me." He screamed at me, "I knew I shouldn't have married you." and proceeded not to speak to me for a week.

Now, our disagreements before the marriage would be explosive at times (*another flag*). I'm pretty laid back and will let you rant and rave until you get too harsh, then I will give it right back to you. He was the type to be brutal and confrontational, if challenged. He felt he was always right as he constantly told me. He wanted to be the man and wear the pants. Because of my upbringing and culture I was happy to let him be in charge. That's what my mother taught me. That was definitely the wrong lesson. I had to eventually learn that if you aren't able to back up your talk and be *"THE MAN"* of the house, then I have to step up and handle the business. Jeff had experienced a lot of hard times in his life, so I gave him lots of breaks and gave in to his temper tantrums. I overlooked his bad moods, outbursts and chalked it up to stress. A month after we were married two things happened. His teaching contract wasn't renewed and his ex-wife also moved out of state and wouldn't let him see his son at all. She had good enough reason though. He was thousands of dollars behind in child support. Sadly, he was also living in a home that financially belonged to my girls and me. We couldn't afford to move anywhere else and purchase our own home because he had no money coming in. No part of his life was going well and I felt bad for him. The train we had boarded together pulled into the station, made its final stop and for the duration of our marriage, he NEVER found full time employment again. That became a big strain on me. Now, I became the head of household again with another dependent.

Since I was working fulltime, I would ask him "Would you help out and just keep the house in order." He scolded me with, "That was a woman's responsibility." He refused to do any work around the house: no cleaning, no cooking, no laundry...nothing. He became a lazy, moody, angry, combative egotistical male where every little thing that was said or done sent him spinning into violent outbursts. I soon became worried that he might turn his anger toward my girls. They liked him in the beginning but now after *"Mr. Hyde"* surfaced, they despised him. They could see and hear how he was treating me (*cursing and calling me all kinds of names*) and the bad part about it was that I continued to take it. I began *"coaching"* the girls on how to act around him and kept them away from him as much as I could.

They became prisoners in their bedrooms and were scared to come out when he was at home.

When my daughters' friends came around, he was so rude and insulting to them. He would always find reasons why he didn't like them. I made excuses for his rudeness and made apologies for him to their friends. He would always throw it in my face that *"Your girls are beneath me. You and your daughters will never be on my level."* He felt he had more education than we did, so he was better than everybody else. Granted, education is a wonderful thing but when you use it to put yourself on a pedestal, to me, you are just an educated fool. Around this time my family and friends also stopped visiting us. My mom and dad told me, "We don't like the way he's treating you and our granddaughters." It was difficult for them to pretend that everything was fine. They decided it was best not to visit at all.

Jeff became very vocal about how I had raised my girls and compared his mother's style of parenting to mine. See, I believe in giving and showing my daughters love and affection even when discipline is necessary. His Mom on the other hand ruled with an iron fist with no thoughts of her children's feelings. If you are yelling and screaming at a child, what lesson are they learning? He wanted me to chastise the girls in front of him instead of in private. He said, "The harder you are on a child the better the child would be." He felt his mother's way was more effective. I disagreed with him whole-heartedly. This led to even more disagreements and fights. Here's another flag and lesson for you. It is crucial that a couple talk about various issues and topics (finances, raising children, where you will live, chores/task-sharing, religion, values, sex,). They should be discussed prior, and not after you're married, so both of you can come to some type of agreement on how those issues/items will be dealt with.

I tried placating him and the girls, making sure that everyone was always happy, but nothing helped. It's not easy playing both sides of the fence trying to be a pleaser. I prayed every night that our *"blended"* family would mesh together and we could all get along. I was totally miserable and didn't know what to do to *"fix"* everything and make things *"right."*

Three months and twenty-two days after we were married, Jeff put his hands on me in a heated argument for the first time. *Did it really matter whether it was in anger or not?* Tell your daughters that under no circumstances, is a man supposed to put his hands on you physically, PERIOD! The argument was stupid. It was over the television being on after midnight in the bedroom. The volume was always loud. I needed to get some sleep because I had to get up early for work (4 a.m.). I asked him "Do you mind going into the living room to watch your movies." We bickered back and forth until he yelled, "Everything you say is bullshit!" I stated earlier "When someone gets too harsh with me or pushes me too hard, I fight back. So, I yelled back *"Fuck you!"* In that instant he threw the T.V. remote control and pounced on me quickly, grabbing my neck and squeezing it as hard as he could (*I felt like a rag doll*). It didn't dawn on me that I was being strangled. My breaths became shorter and shorter and all I could think about was that my daughters were in the house. I was afraid that they would hear or see what was going on and how it would affect them. In my first marriage they had witnessed their dad pushing and shoving me around. I certainly didn't want them to experience that again.

I can remember scratching and digging my fingernails deep into Jeff's hands until he let me go but that was only for a brief moment. He grabbed me and began choking me again to get his point across. He wanted me to know that he was in charge. After gasping desperately for air he finally let me go and stormed out of the room. I ran into the garage in my pajamas to get away from him. I got into the car, closed the door, placed the key into the ignition and turned it on. I looked through the rear view mirror and noticed Jeff was coming after me. I saw the look on his face. It was evil and frightening. I was scared and wanted to escape what I thought would be a bloody deadly ending. I put the car in reverse and wound up backing the car into the garage door before it was totally opened. Jeff ran behind the car so I couldn't leave. If only I had been thinking I would have run his ass over and gone straight to the police station. I just sat in the car with the doors locked waiting for him to go back into the house. Once he did that, I got out of the car and walked outside in the cold and rain crying hysterically. I begged God to tell me what to do. Why didn't I kick him out? Why didn't I call the police? Why didn't I tell someone what was going on? Where was my dignity and self-esteem? I'm not sure. Maybe, I had swept it under the rug like I had done all the other mess he created. All of those questions were in vain...because The next day I forgave him instantly without any reservations. I took total responsibility for his actions and decided that the whole incident was my fault. Why? I think it was a combination of my self-esteem being broken in my first marriage and now this one. I was constantly being told by Jeff "Everything you do is wrong. You can't do anything right." I started believing it. I had already been through one bad marriage and I didn't want to fail again. I can't believe I'm saying this but "I loved this man and really wanted our marriage to work. I had high hopes for us. I was not going to give up. I decided that I was going to be the martyr and take the *"hits for the team."*

Can you believe that following day we went to church? He acted like nothing ever happened. Jeff and the pastor of the church we attended were good friends. Jeff could do no wrong in the pastor's eyes. The pastor was pretty much a chauvinist and expected women to obey their husbands. He was always preaching to women about how the bible says, "Women should honor and obey their husbands." He spoke of women's attitudes and how our position of wanting to wear the pants in the family was not our role. What is wrong with some of these ministers and what "God" do they serve? This is why pastors turn a lot of people away from attending church. Who wants to hear that bullshit about women obeying and serving their men? Who is going to serve us? I wanted to tell the minister about the way Jeff was treating me but since they were friends I felt that he would have sided with him and the pastor would blame me, so I never told him. Plus Jeff would have taken it out on an already brow beaten body.

By this time, I was conditioned to believe I was the problem and I was always doing something wrong to upset Jeff. I tried to say as little as possible to keep the peace. What peace? Maybe that was the problem. I should have made my complaints known. I kept hoping things would improve for Jeff so he would calm down, and hopefully things would get better for us. That never happened. The situation was totally out of control. Things were just crazy in my household. There was no harmony at all. Anytime we were together I was always afraid of Jeff's next outburst. I became hypersensitive to his moods and found myself walking on eggshells constantly, being careful of what I was saying and how I was saying it. Walking on eggshells was a game I played with myself to see if I could keep the calm and peace and avoid disturbing "the monster and breaking the yolk."

Jeff's inner pain and miserable life was projected outward toward me, and my daughters on an almost daily basis. The anger, the insults, the criticism and the callous indifference were draining me on every level. He could not handle that his life was falling apart. His insecurities led him to tear me down in order to build himself up. No matter how hard I tried to make wrongs right, he would still find a reason to grab me, slap me, and call me a "fucking bitch" at the drop of a hat. He would just look at me with anger. Fear would automatically run through me almost paralyzing me. You've heard the phrase *"if looks could kill?"* Well, they were killing me slowly inside. I really began studying him and his foul moods. I learned how to handle him (*Why should anyone have to learn how to handle someone?*) so that I could keep my sanity or what was left of it.

One day we were in the car and he became extremely angry. There was never a valid reason just because he could. He started cursing at me so badly I actually had an out of body experience. Literally, I left my body. I checked out momentarily. I was looking down into the car at us arguing. I could see his words battering me like fists. I remember getting out of the car later feeling so heavy and hopeless.

There were many days that I would come home from work and Jeff hadn't showered or shaved. Sometimes he would still be in his pajamas on the couch. I could tell he had not looked for work that day. I knew his day was spent playing video games and watching porn on-line. I know because he would show me the movies. He said, "I want you to see what other women are doing to satisfy their man and maybe you could learn something from them with your no fucking self." Verbally, he broke me down with his words until I felt like the most unsexiest woman in the world. Engaging in sex with Jeff was always hostile, not tender or loving at all. It felt like I was being used for his therapeutic release or a semen bank. I handled his mental and physical abuse by closing up emotionally. Sex became a chore for me. There was no feeling on my part anymore. I was emotionally detached.

I became invisible in my own space. I was superficial. I kept everything from Jeff. I didn't talk to him about anything dealing with the house (*since it was mine*), my daughters or me. Any business that I allowed him to know about had to be discussed when the girls were not at home. I even got to a point where I didn't even speak to my friends or family when he was around. My only thought was to protect my daughters and to make him happy so he would stop being angry all the time. The reality of this statement is that you cannot make anyone happy. That person must be happy with himself/herself first. This is a major lesson to teach our girls!

There was no pleasing him. Nothing I did was right in Jeff's eyes. He continued verbally attacking everything I did from how I drove the car, cooked, talked on the phone to my friends, and my interactions with my daughters. These were all subjects of long discussions about how I needed to improve and that I had no clue of how to be a good mother to my children.

The stress of it all caused me to gain about 20 pounds. That proposed another problem because he *"hated"* fat women. He had the nerve to tell me "Even though you've gained weight, I'll still fuck you." Those were his exact words. There was no *"making love"* in his world. Eating food was my comfort and escape. I ate boxes of Triscuits, bags of chips, brownies and drank lots of coffee to swallow down my anger and sadness.

Speaking of fat I must divert for a moment. I need to stress the importance of self-esteem and positive body image (*another lesson*) and how some men (*if allowed*) can strip it from you with ease. I was watching a late night talk show centered around a panel of men bashing women on national television. The topic was "Women's Body Parts: What looks good or not? If the woman didn't look good or sexy, would the men tolerate them or get rid of them or keep them? Like a pet? Can you believe that? How demeaning. The show had invited a plastic surgeon as a guest to respond to any questions the men had about women's *imperfections*. One of the questions posed was *"Would you date a woman with sagging breasts?"* There were five men on the panel and three out of the five said they would make their girlfriend or wife get surgery or implants. One of the men said he paid for his girlfriend to have breast surgery and guess what? Soon after the surgery she left him for another man. I found myself cheering and laughing hysterically while thinking he got exactly what he deserved. The moderator asked "What about the belly fat either before or after having a baby?" Four out of the five panelists said, "I would not tolerate it. My woman would have to do something about it by getting plastic surgery or working out at the gym." I couldn't believe my ears. Oh, wait, it gets better. The next question was, "What about stretch marks?" Well, two out of the five said, "Something would have to be done about getting rid of them." The plastic surgeon informed them that, "Stretch marks are scars." The man who bought the boobs for his woman said, "Well, she's going to have to use some cocoa butter or cream to get rid of them or I won't stay with her." He just didn't get it. Trying to remove them surgically would only cause more scarring. No matter how many different ways the surgeon tried to explain it to him, he didn't get it. What an idiot! Two of the guys said, "If my girlfriend or wife got them due to pregnancy, I would accept this because she was having a baby for me." I guess if you weren't having a baby and had stretch marks you would just be SOL (*shit out of luck*). Never was there any talk from these shallow men about inner beauty or how they could be supportive of their girlfriends' or wives' social or emotional issues they may be dealing with. It was all about the physical. I was appalled because there was no talk about what the woman wanted or if she was even happy with the skin she was in. The final straw was the debate over the difference between being thick or fat. The men all agreed that if a woman describes herself as being thick, then more than likely she was shapely. Thick to them meant the woman was physically built. The males on the talk show believed *"a thick woman"* has a big shapely behind and a tiny waist. That was it! I couldn't take anymore. I turned the program and T.V. off. Is this what entertainment has come to, critiquing women's bodies? The irony is the men on the program were no prizes. None of them were a match for the perfect Mr. America. They had a lot of nerve being allowed to define what beauty is. This kind of propaganda and bashing is destructive and encourages girls/women to do harm to their bodies in order to please their men, husbands, and boyfriends. We, as mothers, must ensure that our daughters are well equipped to handle these kinds of attacks and propaganda on their appearance, self-confidence, self-esteem and well-being. We must continue to build a nation of strong women who are safe and secure with whom they are.

After all the things Jeff had said and done to me I gave serious thought to shooting him in his sleep, stabbing him in his back or poisoning his ass and dragging him to the woods to die. No matter how badly he continued to treat me, I still made dinner everyday and fixed his plate like a dutiful wife. Poisoning him could have been a viable option and it would have been easy to do.

The really bad part for me was how he treated his female friends. I would hear him talking to them on the telephone and they always got kind words and praise. They seemed to have fun and enjoyed each other's company. The nicest thing he ever said to me once the abuse started was "You really do laundry well. At least I always have clean clothes. You are good at that."

The last time he put his hands on me was Valentine's Day. We had an argument about sex. He would "critique" me every time we had sex. *(I now know that he was insecure of his own performance).* As far as I was concerned I was fine in the bedroom. I giggled sometimes silently because I would get nervous. I always wanted things to be *"right"* sexually *(stupid me)*. Well, Valentine's Day night he called me a "silly trick bitch." And, I snapped. He snapped right back. He started hitting me on the side of my head, hitting my arms and hands with his fist. As I reached for the phone to call for help he hit me in my chest. I dropped the phone and we physically fought like we were in a boxing ring. At the end of the fight, I had a tender spot on the side of my face, a bruise over my left breast and right forearm and my fingernails were all ripped. I was so devastated. I went outside in my nightgown and bare feet (Remember, this is February.) to call my best friend. I had to tell somebody. I knew something had to change. I could no longer be around him. He had proven that he didn't love, respect or cherish me. He didn't have my back. He didn't have the girls' best interest at heart either. I no longer wanted him in my life.

It took four months from that day of praying and visualizing him out my house. Sometimes you have to just pray a man out of your life just like you prayed him in. He finally found and accepted a full time job in upstate New York and left. I don't know what would have happened if he hadn't gotten that job. The months between Valentine's Day night and Jeff leaving for his new job were pure hell.

I have no idea how I managed to put up with him. I know this might sound crazy, but he had an evil smell emanating from his body. It was like his anger and evilness were seeping through his pores. My whole house smelled bad because of him. I just kept apologizing to my girls for what I had brought into our house. I felt that I scarred them once again after putting them through the trauma and divorce with their father and now I was doing it again with Jeff.

Jeff was verbally, mentally, physically cruel and abusive to me. I didn't deserve that. I still get angry with myself sometimes for wasting so much time on a marriage that was so one-sided. I'm angry with myself for allowing this man to come into my home and destroy my daughters' lives and mine. I'm angry that I allowed Jeff to put his hands on me thinking it was okay. I'm angry he didn't have his shit together after three years of marriage and he had the nerve to blame it all on me? My divorce was final fifteen months ago. I'm $36,000 dollars poorer for all the money I poured into our marriage. I suffer from horrible anxiety attacks. I have weird eating habits, stress and my weight to deal with but I would rather deal with that than Jeff.

I look back over my life and realized in both of my former marriages, that my husbands weren't in love with me even though I was crazy about them. I guess that's why a lot of the older women say, *"Always get with a man that loves you more."* My husbands both married me because I am a *"good"* woman, who would take care of them and make their lives easier. They both behaved as if they *"settled"* with me and I was only there to wait on them hand and foot. Since they were not totally happy being with me, their mindset eventually became disgruntled and abusive. The first man I loved was mentally and verbally hurtful. The second one was physically, verbally and mentally abusive. I will not allow myself to be in a situation again where the man thinks he didn't really get what he wanted and just settled with me to get by. From now on, any man involved with me will have to kiss the ground I walk on and that's the lesson learned.

I used to wonder what love really is or does it even exist. According to the dictionary love is a verb, doing something for someone and not just saying it. Why do people bother to say, *"I love you"* if there is no physical action behind it? What is the point? I still believe in love and romance. I know that eventually I will be in a committed and loving relationship with a wonderful man. I feel that. I know that I still have work to do on myself. I want to trust men, but in the back of my mind I wonder, *"Should they be trusted?"* I will learn in time to release the pain from my two unsuccessful marriages and I will begin dating at some point in my life. I need to get my head together by rebuilding my self-worth first. My self-confidence is getting stronger which indicates that I am healing. I see it in my thinking and behavior.

I'm so glad that I explained to my daughters from the time they were teenagers that, "You might have to kiss a lot of frogs before you meet "Mr. Right." It is important for our girls to understand that if they have been emotionally abused in a relationship, they will need to let go, regroup, and refresh before starting a new one. If you don't regroup and start fresh, it is possible that you could sabotage the next possible relationship. You cannot hold onto old baggage packed with fears, insecurities, hurt, and negative self-talk and put it in the new luggage.

I did express to my daughters to *"Be guarded."* That means do not enter into any relationship with your eyes closed. Determine, from the beginning of a relationship, what you're willing and not willing to accept. If you cannot be treated with the respect you deserve, move on. Unfortunately it doesn't always work like that. It's not always that simple because a little four letter word often times gets in the way called *"love."* This one word sometimes makes people do some crazy things. That's why it's important to be clear about your self worth and love yourself. Know who you are and what you are willing to accept.

I have talked to my daughters over and over again about what to look for in a man and how they should behave in various situations. Remember, sometimes men will misrepresent who they are and try to fool you. They might be one way while they are dating you and change once the relationship progresses. This doesn't just apply to men but anyone that enters your life.

They know before they can go out with someone that I want to meet them first. A mother should know who their daughter(s) are engaging or considering for dating or entering into a relationship with. That poor young man will feel some heat from me. It's only because I never want my daughters' or any woman for that matter to go through the ordeals that I did (*not to say that it won't happen*). I can't follow them around for the rest of their lives stalking them but I can sure try. If I learned one thing from this hellacious experience it was, "Don't waste your time sitting around waiting for others to change.

## CHANGE YOUR SELF! SAVE YOURSELF!

I had to do some deep exploration of who I am. What kind of woman could put her daughters and herself through this nightmare? The answer hit me like a ton of rocks. I'm a pleaser! What a pleaser does is commit herself/himself to boosting the well-being of other people even while compromising their own emotional, physical, or economical status. I had sacrificed my own wants and needs to accommodate him. My agenda became his agenda. What about me? There was no me. I just wanted to get along and please him.

### "Don't Be A Please Him...Be a Please Her"

How does one evolve to becoming a pleaser? It begins during childhood when parents tell their kids what they should and shouldn't do, never allowing them to think for themselves or make decisions. A child learns that if she/he obeys their parents rewards are given. The rewards may be love, approval, acceptance or material items. If the children disobey, the consequences could be punishment (*verbal, mental, physical or emotional*). Which one would you choose? The child starts to feel worthy by pleasing their parents and others. They don't want to feel unloved. They are willing to fulfill the expectations requested so they can be accepted and loved. Tell your daughters "Don't ever sacrifice the value of their self-worth to appease or please anyone.

Don't be a welcome mat for friends, co-workers, bosses, relatives, and never ever for a man.

### Self Esteem 101

The formative years are the most important in the intellectual and social-emotional development of a child. Unfortunately, our daughters are not born with self-esteem. We have to teach that to them. During this growth stage she will develop self-confidence, learn about empathy, nurturing, security, and how to give and accept love. The best teacher and role model will be you.

As your daughter(s) transition into the adolescent stages, they will be given more opportunities to handle challenging and new responsibilities and situations. They will learn to trust themselves, make decisions/choices on their own that will aid and prepare them for adulthood.

Our daughters today are faced with many pressures. Their "*To Do*" list is endless. They want to fit in (*a need to belong or be popular*), adhere to societies expectations (*of what and who they say they should be*), feel pretty, develop their talents and compete for boys'/men's attention (*We don't like this one but get ready it's inevitable*). Help your daughter(s) to value themselves. Involve her father, male relative(s), or mentor(s) to focus on *"who"* she is on the inside, and not just the outer appearance.

> ➤ Remember, the father is your daughter's first admirer. Hopefully, he will educate her on balancing the powers within male and female relationships. If there are no positive male role model(s) for our daughter(s), moms or other women then we must accept and execute the tasks at hand ourselves.
>
> ➤ Encourage her to maintain a "Can-Do" attitude toward challenging tasks and participate in activities that promote diverse interests. This will increase her self- confidence.
>
> ➤ Tell them that their abilities are equal to males. They are not bound or locked into gender-dominated fields. They have the right to choose.
>
> ➤ Listen to "what they say or have said." Respect their ideas, thoughts and opinions. Our daughters will make mistakes along the way but with our support, guidance and opportunities to improve their decision making skills will build their self-confidence to make appropriate choices.
>
> ➤ Start at an early age teaching them to love their bodies and refute the social forces that dictate to "Look a certain way in order to be beautiful and successful." Let her know she doesn't have to be perfect and no one is.
>
> ➤ Help her to set realistic and achievable goals by focusing on her intelligence, skills and talents. She will feel good about herself when she is able to meet her goals and improve *her* self-esteem.
>
> ➤ Be a role model and include other positive female role models. Motivate and encourage our daughters. Continue to send consistent positive messages.

Positive phrases that heal will build self-esteem and confidence in our girls. This checklist will help.

### ✓ The List

* Listen to a Higher Power
* Respect self/others
* Encourage self to improve self
* Accept self
* Give PRAISE & THANKS to a
Higher Power
* Avoid being judgmental to self /others
* Be supportive to others
* Nurture self
* Make "Quality Time" for self
* Motivate self
* Communicate needs to self/and others
* Hug self
* Smile

### *Dream...Esteem*

I finally have peace in my home again. My girls are grown and doing their own things. They still bring their male friends home for me to meet and I try not to give them the third degree. The bottom line is my girls can never say ...

**"Mama didn't teach us!"**

*three*

# A High Roller Who Lost It All

"I became a high roller at age 20. I was
selling drugs to NFL's athletes. I was making
big money and spending it just as fast up
my nose. I broke the sacred creed in the
game. I became my biggest customer.

*Maria Chelsey 31 years old, Chicago, Illinois*

I grew up in a household of nine. Gina, my mother, raised us
alone. Education was never a high priority for us. I guess she
didn't understand that education was "not only the key to
unlock the doors to freedom" but also to "unlock the mind."
Her education took her from an honor student in high school
to Community College She never finished but at least she went.
That's why I could never understand why she didn't teach us or
stress the importance of school. There was never any encouragement for us to complete high school or pursue a higher education. We could go *or* not go and there was no penalty if we
didn't. Maybe she was just too tired to think about it raising all
these kids and figuring out how to feed us. This was the beginning of me learning that I could pretty much do what I wanted
and when I wanted to.

I missed out on the part where there were consequences in life for one's behavior, good or bad, and how this *understanding* applies to the decisions and choices that are made on a daily basis. Later on I would learn some valuable lessons the hard way. Gina's philosophy was pretty simple; *"You're on your own."* Her outlook was to live your life by trial and error. It is so important that a child be taught at an early age *right* from *wrong*, if not they will fall to error and that's exactly what I did. Now, I'm not saying that just because a mother teaches her child right from wrong, he/she will grow up to be an angel. However parents should lay the foundation and plant positive seeds for their children to grow on.

My mom's solutions for our misbehaviors were to beat us with whatever she could get her hands on literally. She never took the time to explain our wrong doings or how we could have chosen to do things differently. It was not instilled in us that we always had a choice. I came to the conclusion that it was simpler to just be a follower that way you didn't have to think much. I began watching what everybody else did and that's what I would do. Sometimes, being a follower can lead you places where you don't need to go. I took Gina's advice and realized that I had to learn how to play the game of life on my own. Remember, Mama said, *"trial and error."*

In high school I basically just hung out. I didn't go to class much since it wasn't a priority or valued. School was more of a social experience for me. Thanks to mama I did pretty much what I wanted. I decided who my friends would be, I came home when I got ready, I didn't have a curfew and I stayed out as late and long as I wanted.

There is an old saying that, "Nothing good ever happens after midnight." I found that to be very true. When you're in the streets with no purpose, anything can happen. The only time Gina would say something about curfew was when the neighbors complained and brought it to her attention. They would ring the doorbell and ask her "Why aren't your kids in the house?" We were on the block (*neighborhood*) just hanging out late at night when we should have been in the house doing homework. She would come outside and yell, "Ya'll get in this house!" As soon as the neighbors went back into their houses, we were right back on the streets again. There was no structure for us.

Everything that shaped my life from nine years on started with Steve. I had known him most of my life. We were always together. I guess you could say we had a crush on each other. As we got older we hung out and throughout school I was always his girl. I was young and dumb. I say that because I never received the *"Mother Talk"* about boys, relationships, drugs, and especially sex. I didn't know in from out. Steve and I had been running buddies, which it seemed like forever and as the years went by we eventually got married. I was (18) and he was (21). On the day I said, *"I do"* I had no idea why I was getting married. I guess because everybody expected it. After all, he was the only man I had ever known. It was always just Steve and me. That became my answer and rationale. At the time I didn't realize I had other options and I never entertained them. There were many other things that I could have done beside get married. I could have graduated from high school, attended college and graduated or pursued some other type of career training. No one was pushing me and I wasn't pushing myself either. I knew Steve had messed around with other women and experimented from time to time with drugs but he was all I ever had, so I married him anyway.

A year later, I was pregnant with my first child because I didn't have enough sense to use birth control. It never crossed my mind. That is a discussion Gina and I never had. Like I said, "I didn't know in from out so a few years later I became pregnant again. I'm not saying that I wasn't happy or I didn't love my children but I didn't have to start so young. That's why you have to learn early how to make decisions and choices that are wise.

One night I was invited to a friend's birthday party. Steve didn't go but I did. When I walked through the door you could see drug dealers near and far. Of course they had brought party favors with them for everyone. In fact, there was so much dope it could have filled a bathtub. You would have thought *"Scarface"* was throwing the party. I was hanging tough with the best of them indulging in all the dope that was available. A follower will do most anything so I tried a couple of lines of cocaine up my nose trying to get high but nothing happened. It did not seem to have an affect on me. It wasn't working. You would have thought good sense would have kicked in and made me stop right then, but I just kept trying. I wanted to be like everybody else. It actually took about a month of snorting before I was finally hooked.

In case you don't understand, any drug that you start using whether it is cigarettes, alcohol, or whatever your poison may be, becomes a gateway to the next drug. Consuming so much cocaine sent me to another level. I started smoking *primos,* which is a combination of coke and weed. My good sense never kicked in and now I had graduated to the world of addiction.

The choices I made and the drugs I took did not come cheap. There was a price to pay. In order to survive and keep up with my habit I learned quickly how to become a schemer, always hustling and thinking up scams to get over. I was just trying to make a quick buck to keep getting high. Unfortunately, I was my biggest customer. I made money at little low level jobs but I would turn around and give it right back to the dealer and up my nose. There's one thing I can say about Steve he was a functional user. He didn't have to be high all the time and that's how he was able to keep a job.

Later on, I got my first opportunity and training (*that I would be able to use later*) working during the night selling drugs with the neighborhood boys and in time made enough money to start my own little business. It helped to pay the bills and it kept my high going. People were at my house all the time (*as I look back now I can't believe I put my kids in jeopardy with addicts coming and going*). They were always hanging around waiting for the store to open (*the drug store*).

I became greedy and there were times when I stole small amounts of dope from my drug connections to get high with. That takes a lot of nerve. I thought I was slick but believe me, this was not a smart move. When you mess with other peoples' money you are messing with their livelihood; their reputation and you are flirting first hand with danger. It will get you beat up, hurt, injured or even killed. They were much smarter and slicker than me so I experienced that beat down on numerous times but that didn't slow me down. What were a few bruised eyes, black and blue marks on your body when you're making big bank! I was still spending the money almost as fast as I was making it and I finally got dealt out of the game which was really a good thing because Steve was tired of my lifestyle and the people hanging around the house. It was illegal, dangerous and it put our kids safety at risk.

Now, I was unable to support my own habit and that's when I hit an all time low of degradation and humiliation. I started begging for drugs from anybody and everybody to get high. In case you don't know anything about drugs, as times goes by you need more and more to get high. Your body builds up a tolerance or immunity, which requires you to consume more of the substance. When you are using, days turn into weeks, weeks turn into months and before you know it, your life becomes a blur. The drugs had a hold on me. I was just out there in a fog.

I remember once leaving home to get high knowing my kids would be left alone. (*Steve was working nights and expected me to be home*) On my way out the door my daughter yelled, "Mama, you forgot your razor and straw on the table!" Imagine the shock I felt hearing my young daughter telling me not to forget my paraphernalia. It was like she was telling me not to forget my purse or hat. This was a startling wake up call and a stab in my heart. I was stunned but that didn't stop me from going to get that next high. I still wondered how many times she had watched me using and I never even noticed. What kind of impression was I making in her life and what was I teaching her?

I realized that I had committed the worse crime of all, negligence. Do you think that had any impact on my conscious? Do you think that stopped me? No, I continued to go down the road of disaster until I hit rock bottom. What does that mean? It means I didn't care anymore about anything. My personal appearance was an indication of that. I didn't care how I looked. My hair was not combed. My clothes were wrinkled. I was just sloppy. I didn't care about anything except where my next high was coming from. This behavior finally cost me to lose my kids. My husband was doing a little bit better than me, (*he was working as a mechanic in a neighborhood auto shop*). He had to step in and take charge. I was incapable of making any rational decisions. I was physically unable to care for them. I was sucking up the money that Steve gave me to run the house. I wasn't working so financially I couldn't help feed and clothe my kids or myself. Even though Steve was doing drugs (*weed*) too he wasn't hooked like me. One day after he came home from work he told me that he couldn't take it anymore because there was more money going out than was coming in. He warned me to get it together and get some help.

One night when I stumbled home high and put my key in the door I soon discovered that I couldn't get in. What Steve had told me rang in the back of my mind. He had changed the locks and put all of my personal belongings in the back yard. All the knocking and banging on the door did not make it open so I went to a friend's house that night not too far away and moved in for a short time She made it very clear that it would be for a short time. After all, who wants to live with a drug addict except another drug addict. Not even my mother would take me in.

When I was able to somewhat pull myself together I would find part time jobs here and there (*between getting high*). I always told my oldest kid to meet me at work on payday so I could give them a few dollars for extra things they needed. If they didn't get there by the time I was ready to leave work they never would see it. That cash would go straight up my nose.

Steve could see I was in a bad situation. He felt sorry for me and allowed me to come back several times in hopes that I would get some help but it was just a matter of time before we would finally break up. He was verbally and physically abusive to me and was still hanging out with other women. There was really nothing holding our marriage together. There was definitely no future in two druggies staying together. Steve took care of the kids for a while but the responsibilities of raising a family and taking care of the house became too much for him. He wasn't making a lot of money and he was smoking more than he used to. That's when my mother agreed to step in and take care of them. I don't know why cuz she certainly didn't take care of me but none of us wanted them taken into DCFS custody. I believe her guilt was what made her make that decision. Whatever the reason she did it so it was a done deal.

Several months went by and I had straightened up my act a little bit again. I was still working little jobs here and there and I had started fixing myself up. (*I was almost looking like my old self again but I was still using*). The friend I was staying with lost her job (*last hired first fired*). With no income for the rent and me with nothing to add she had to leave her apartment. She was able to move in with a relative but that didn't help me any. She couldn't take me with her so I was on the street living hand to foot wherever I could.

It didn't take long for me to find another means to my end. When you're desperate enough you will do something. I became attracted to a dope dealer that I knew from my past that lived in the area and he took me in. He began taking care of me but with that came a price (*if you know what I mean*). He was my comfort and security or at least I thought so. I always had a lack of self-worth and self-esteem. I had not been taught the basic lessons of womanhood (*to love yourself*) and so I continued to draw physical abusers into my life. I had no clue of how a man was supposed to treat a woman, and I certainly didn't know what my role was as a woman. This particular relationship turned out to be no different. What I thought started out to be a positive situation for me turned into a bad situation. I allowed this man to strip away every bit of dignity that I might have had left. He made a constant fool out of me. He did this by humiliating me on a daily basis in front of his family and friends (calling me a junkie and jumping on me just for the heck of it. He would physically and verbally abuse me. It was a sport for him. His friends and family thought I was their personal entertainment. Since he was supplying my habit, I was under is control. I did what he told me to do and when to do it.

I knew I couldn't continue to live like this because either he would kill me or I would kill him. I started looking and applying for jobs in hopes of leaving this negative environment. The job hunt was not easy considering I had little education, no skills and I was a user. Talking to some people in my neighborhood I managed to find out about a job opening in a health care agency as a companion for senior citizens. I took a few days to clean up my act and get myself together before I interviewed with the agency. They seemed very pleased with me and actually offered me the job. There is one skill that I did have (*I knew how to bullshit and manipulate people*). It was only minimum wage but what do you expect with minimum education and minimum skills. There was only one problem and it was a big one. How would I pass the drug test? Being the schemer I was, I enlisted one of my relatives to provide me with a sample of their urine. At the lab I took the aspirin bottle that was given to me into the bathroom and poured my cousins urine into the jar and returned it to the lab technician. A few days later I was gainfully employed. I couldn't have been happier because I was finally able to escape the hell- hole I had been living in.

It was the perfect set up for me. I had my own room and all I had to do was act as a companion and perform a few jobs around the house. My responsibilities for Mrs. Jacobs was to help her cook, do some light housekeeping, help her get dressed, and make sure she took her proper medication. This was not a difficult job to perform. I was basically in charge of the household. I was only there (4) days a week and one of her relatives came and stayed with her on her on my off days.

My day as a companion was pretty easy. I discovered that the longer I was there, the more comfortable I became. It has been said, *"An idle mind is the devil's workshop."* That was true in my case. I was on duty for twenty-four hours a day. There is only so much work to do in that time span. I became bored and started getting high in her house. I was still hustling when I could, trying to make a fast dollar to get high. There was always one scam after another (*writing bad checks or whatever I could find to do*).

One day I was looking out the window and noticed a suitcase in the next-door neighbor's driveway unattended. No one was claiming it or seemed to be concerned. It was just sitting there. I was curious so I went over there to investigate. I opened the suitcase and found that it was filled with jewelry. All I could do was say, "This is my lucky day." There was a card inside the luggage with a contact number. I called the number to let them know "I had found the luggage (*that was a dumb move*)." When you're high you're not thinking rationally. Fortunately for me no one ever returned my call and thus began my next hustle.

In the meantime I needed to get high. I immediately grabbed a few pieces of the jewelry and made my way to the nearest pawnshop not too far away from Mrs. Jacobs's home. I thought I had just stumbled on some cheap costume jewelry. When I gave some of the pieces to the shopkeeper I was totally surprised when he said "I'll give you $200.00 for this." You know what that meant. I could afford all the drugs I could handle until it ran out. I sold the jewelry, got the money, located some drugs and got high.

A few days later my cousin came over to Mrs. Jacobs home and took some more of the jewelry to be appraised only at a different pawnshop. We figured it wouldn't be wise to return to the same shop. We needed to know how much the rest of the jewelry was worth. This would determine if we were going to buy some more drugs to sell or just get high. On that particular day I had to attend a funeral. After the service I went back to work to wait for further word from my cousin about the appraisal of the remaining jewelry. As I was getting high, I heard a knock at the door. Surprise! It was the police. When I opened the door, they pushed their way in with guns drawn ready to shoot. I asked them "What the problem was?" They told me they had a warrant for my arrest. When I made the phone call to the number I found on the card in the suitcase to report that some jewelry had been found, they traced the call back to me. I made the call from the house so they knew exactly where to find me. When my cousin took the jewelry to be appraised, the owners had already reported it as stolen to the police. They had contacted the few pawnshops in the area and they were able to find it. I found out later that in their rush to leave they forgot to put the luggage in the car. They had called one of their neighbors and were told the luggage was gone. The police immediately handcuffed me and took me jail. My cousin was already locked up and I was in there for at least eighteen hours before my uncle came to bail us out.

On the day that I was to appear in court, I was a nervous wreck. All I could think about was *"if I'm going to be locked up" "how will I get high?"* Fortunately, they threw the case out because I cooperated with the police and I didn't have a prior record. All the jewelry was recovered and returned to the rightful owners and they chose not to press charges because they were close to their neighbor Ms. Jacobs (*they didn't want to upset her since she was elderly*). They were just happy to get their jewelry back. I did have to pay the $200.00 back to the pawnshop. Boy, did I catch a blessing! But that didn't stop me from getting high. No way!

My employment with the healthcare agency of course ended after the arrest but I came up with other little hustles to make money. During this time I started cleaning up my act again (*it's always again and again until you stop*). I started dressing better, getting my hair and nails done and putting some distance between me and the *caine*. Somehow, I always seemed to land on my feet and another opportunity soon became available to me. It was an addict's dream. I had an opportunity to sell drugs to professional football players. I was able to make a connection through a friend of mine (*who was a trainer*) with a high profile dealer who cut me in on the cocaine market. I became the personal shopper for many NFL athletes. I made sure they were well supplied sometimes before and after the games. I was hanging with the big dogs now. I was on top of the world and living large. Even though I made big money, I spent big money. I was still my own *best* and *worst* customer and this does not make for a fruitful business. The dealer (DJ) divided his crew into NFL team regions. It was definitely a business and he ran it like one. He divided his crew into regions so that distribution was equal and everybody got a piece of the action. I traveled all over the United States from Atlanta, Dallas, New Orleans Miami, Houston and Tampa. I would go from state to state like a confectioner selling my sweet candy.

I was also a football fan so it was always exciting going to the games and watching my customers play from the 50-yard line. In the wintertime I was privileged to sit in the club skyboxes. Players paid up to $60,000 for these cozy rooms. They were furnished with a bathroom, a mini kitchen, and flat screen T.V.'s, drinks, and platters and trays of hot and cold food. It was fully carpeted with leather couches and chairs, pure paradise. Stadium staff periodically came in and replenished the refreshments and cleaned the bathroom as needed. I felt just like a celebrity.

All this was sweet but the after parties were sweeter. It didn't matter what city you were in there were always plenty of hoes and groupies waiting to git their party on. A lot of times the players would fly these ladies in for their own pleasure to share with their teammates. The rooms and suites were filled with rookies, veterans, and sometimes entertainers. I know you want to know who these V.I.P.'s were but I can't reveal their names. Not only would I probably have a lawsuit on my hands but it would also hurt a lot of people including their families and I'm not on that!

By the time we would get to the hotel room service had already delivered cases of Cristal (and any other liquor you could ask for) and trays of food. Of course I was there to liven up the party with my dessert (*nose candy*). When I think back it amazes me that I was able to travel effortlessly with plastic bags filled with the desirable white powder right through security. Transporting drugs across state lines is a federal offense. If I had ever been caught I could have been looking at possibly twenty years. Most of the guys started off using about half a gram every four to six weeks and sometimes graduating to more. There were a few that would buy eight balls (that's three grams). I would start off selling a couple thousand dollars worth and then the party would begin. I remember the rooms and suites were packed with all kinds of combinations (*2-3 girls and a guy, monogamous couples, and sometimes groups*). There was always some freaky shit going on. One time I had to go to the bathroom and I walked in on two couples having sex in the shower...damn... smoking, snortin, drinkin and sex. That was the name of the game. I often wondered how these athletes managed to get high and still play at the top of their game. Of course everyone did not manage it well. You would always hear in the news how players failed their random drug checks and would have to go to rehab or be suspended or fired from the league.

As fate would have it, I eventually became part of the game. That was my downfall. Mistake one I started dating an athlete. I won't tell you his name or team because you would definitely know who he is (*I will call him TC.*) he played for a team in the Eastern Conference. I soon learned that it's not good to mix business with pleasure. Mistake two was that I began doing freebees of cocaine with TC and mistake three was that I became obsessed about his womanizing (*What did I expect from dating an athlete?*) Now, don't get me wrong all athletes are not unfaithful or assholes. I found myself spending too much time calling to see where he was and who he was with. It almost became a second job for me and it was so stressful. I was getting high just to keep my sanity. What was it about these lessons that I didn't get? Finally, I had to let TC go and I went back to Chicago a mental and emotional mess!

Oh well the show must go on and days later, it was time for me to go back to work. I arrived at the airport for my flight to Miami to make my usual delivery. I was high and about to go through security when all of a sudden paranoia set in. I looked around and noticed some narcs (*drug agents*) in the security area. I was trained to spot them a mile away. Well, I panicked and rushed out of the line. You never knew if someone had dropped a dime on you. I hurried back to the terminal into the washroom and flushed everything I was carrying down the toilet. I never made it to Miami. Unfortunately, my paranoia took over too many times after that. I was always thinking that someone was watching me and that I was going to get arrested any minute. In the end I was dumping more cocaine than I was delivering. DJ decided that my trafficking days with him were over. I had messed up too much of his money and I wasn't taking care of business like I should have been. I wasn't able to pay D.J. back for all the money I had lost him so he took it out in another way, on my body. I took a beat down that I will never forget. I was his personal punching bag and release for all of his frustrations. I blacked out and when I woke up I was lying in a hospital bed with a fractured jaw, two broken fingers, (*trying to defend myself*) a twisted ankle, and a black eye. I was in the hospital for several weeks before I was discharged. You're probably wondering if I pressed charges against D.J. for the beat down.

Of course I didn't. That would have been suicide considering we were both involved in illegal activities. We would have been looking at some real jail time. I took this experience and chalked it up as another life lesson. A PAINFUL ONE!

You wouldn't think the way my life was going that things could get any worse well it did. The days got darker for me. It's been said, "That death comes in three's." and that's exactly what happened. My best friend died in her sleep from an asthma attack and I lost my cousin to a drug overdose and a child hood friend had a heart attack. Those events caused me to embrace my choice of drugs even more. I felt like I needed something to deaden and numb the pain I was feeling. During this time I believe God was probably trying to tell me something. Three deaths should have been a wake-up call for me. I still didn't get it.

Addicts have a saying "There is no honor among drug addicts." We are always looking for and chasing that next high. Sex for drugs was always a guaranteed option. Women addicts have another saying: "Sex for drugs... a fuck for a buck... make ya holla for a dolla... do something strange for some change... and twenty will get you plenty." I certainly had no honor and was true to the sayings.

I started sleeping with one of my best friend's father. He was always looking for a young *thang* and I wanted it to be me. He got what he wanted. I got what I wanted. We were both happy. We began seeing each other on a regular basis. He started helping me to take care of my kids and me (*they were still staying with my mom*). He was buying them clothes and whatever I wanted or needed. He really stuck by me and supported me. One day we were at his house on the sofa and Rita (*his daughter came through the back door and witnessed one of our make out sessions it turned into an ugly scene*). Of course when my girlfriend found out that I was screwing her daddy, she was not happy and who would be. I really couldn't blame her. Eventually, that hustle came to an end and so did our friendship.

Several times I did attempt to stop my habit. I went through withdrawal. The sweats, shakes, vomiting, and the physical and mental anguish should have been enough for me to say "No more Never again!" No matter how hard I tried, somehow relapse tended to find me and look me straight in my face again. I tried to blame something or somebody for my own downfall but I made the choices and there was no one else to blame but myself.

One night I started looking for something, *ANYTHING* to take me out of my misery. I didn't care what the drug was. I went to a drug spot and ran into a friend's cousin who was a crack addict along with some of the other hypes on the block. I asked them to help me out. They all had heard that I was trying to get clean again. He didn't want to see me out there begging so he refused to give me anything. I kept asking around but nobody was sharing that night. That was nothing but the *GRACE* of God who kept me from getting high.

I was unemployed, broke and had nowhere to live. Another friend of mine wanted to help me and she allowed me to stay with her so that I could get myself together. One evening, she suggested that we both attend her church. They were having a service that night so I agreed to go with her and thank goodness I did. It turned out to be very positive for me. I began to pray and pray. I really wanted to stop and I asked God to take the desire for drugs away from me. What I found out was that faith plus desire are a powerful combination.

There were NO clinics, no methadone, no weekly drops, no counseling nor relapse staring me in my face, just GOD. HE stepped in and healed me from my demons. I am happy to say that I've been clean for ten years and some months. I have not done any drugs since. Hallelujah!!!! I'm free!!!! The church helped me to find a job and a place to stay. I was able to get my kids back and we became a family again. Steve and I divorced but he still keeps in touch and he does spend time with the kids. What happened to the rest of the crowd I used to hang out with? Most of them have met their fate through AIDS, murder, drug overdose, or jail time. Gina has since apologized for not being more supportive and open with me while I was growing up. I guess it hurt her to see what all I went through and still survived. Our relationship continues to improve.

Although Gina could have shared some of her mother wit with me, you still have to take responsibility for your own actions. Growing up is not an easy process. There are no road maps that prepare our daughters for life. We cannot always teach them everything but we can be there to guide them. It should be understood that there are some lessons that you cannot escape. Some things are meant to be but we still have to prepare our daughters as best as we can. The lessons I learned just may help you!

### # 1 Lesson Learned Education

- ➢ Education is a must to become independent and financially secure.
- ➢ Demonstrate/teach that for every good or bad action there are rewards or consequences.
- ➢ Allow one to learn the mistakes of others in hopes that they won't be repeated.
- ➢ Provide the necessary tools to think for self and AVOID following others.
- ➢ Teach them how to handle responsibility.
- ➢ Assist in acknowledging their potential for success.

### #2 Lesson Learned Decision Making

- ➢ When children make inappropriate decisions, discuss with them how and why they made those decisions.
- ➢ When things go wrong discuss how they could have done things differently and look at other possible choices.

- ➢ Instead of punishing/reprimanding (*using verbally abusive language or beating them*) ask "What would you do the next time if a decision has to be made in a similar situation?"
- ➢ Modeling good choices aren't something adults or parents always do but it is important to show our children how things should be done.
- ➢ Share some past decisions that were made that did not turn out well. Allow them to create preventive measures/solutions (ex: *How does one avoid running late for work? If running late for work, what should you do?*).
- ➢ Begin teaching decision-making skills at an early age. Begin allowing a child to make small simple decisions (ex: choice of a fruit/vegetable for a snack, choose an activity/a game to be played, or what story they want to read).
- ➢ Provide frequent opportunities for them to decide between several options. This allows the child to learn how the process of decision-making works. In practicing this process, she will learn that the choices made will determine the consequences received.

As a child becomes older and continues to make choices that are solid she will be allowed to broaden the various decisions that are made (ex: a child who consistently adheres to a designated curfew may be permitted to extend those hours on certain occasions. Rewarding good choices can be a motivating factor for developing a healthy pattern of wise decision- making and responsible behavior.

### "How To Have That Conversation About Drugs"

Before that talk begins, make certain that you are well informed about drugs and its side effects (*mentally, spiritually, emotionally, physically and financially*). It is important how this information is presented. Avoid the approach that comes from an authoritative viewpoint. As soon as you start expressing to them *"You better not be doing drugs!"* or *"I'd better not catch you doing drugs!"* You have already lost them and they have now tuned you out. Asking them questions and providing the basic information about drugs is a better approach.

### *The Check List*

> Ask them, *"What have you heard about drugs?"* or *"What do you know about drugs?"*
> Listen to their responses without interrupting them. *Why?* Listening allows them to know that you are interested in what they have to say. Respect their thoughts and opinions. They will feel comfortable and possibly safe enough to open themselves to you about anything.
> Provide the facts about drugs. They will begin to look at drugs differently. Their attitudes about drugs can change. This will allow them to make conscious choices. We cannot always bet on this happening but at least the foundation has been laid. Here are some facts to share:
> Some teens use drugs to fit in with friends. Boredom, curiosity, and escape from reality are other reasons to experiment with any controlled substance. Drugs DO NOT solve problems!
> Using drugs can lead to addiction. This means your body can't function without them.

Withdrawing from drugs can cause symptoms such as sweating, tremors, shaking, and vomiting. These symptoms will continue until the body is drug free.

Drugs (*legal* or *illegal*) are dangerous for a child or teen's body because their body is still growing. Misuse of drugs or any controlled substance can damage the brain, heart, and other organs. The use of cocaine can cause heart attacks.

> Drug use impairs your ability to think clearly and make wise decisions.

➢ Inappropriate and negative activities could hurt you or others while using drugs.

➢ Drug use can hamper one from doing well in school, sports and other activities.

The road to recovery was not easy for me and I was fortunate that I did not have to seek "in" or "out" patient therapy.

There is an African proverb that sates "Each one teach one." As mothers, we must accept our responsibilities and pass the lessons that we have learned onto our daughters.

The challenges that I experienced provided me with valuable knowledge that I will share with my daughter. Now, whether she listens or not at least I can say

**"You have been warned."**

## *four*

# Money Can't Buy You Love!

"He wore Armani suits, drove a Cadillac, his rent was paid, he slept on satin sheets and he ate in the finest restaurants. There was nothing too good for the men I dated. It took filing bankruptcy and the loss of everything to teach me "Money can't buy you love."

*Samantha Kaufman, 43 years old, Denver, Colorado*

Money, money, money, it doesn't grow on trees. I don't know why my Mom left out that very important lesson and piece of valuable information. I grew up in a two-parent family. Both of them brought home the bacon (*money*). My mother made significantly more than my father but for some reason she felt it was her responsibility to provide and do more for the household. Whoever came up with the theory that "A man is supposed to take care of the home." certainly did not live with my family. In fact, my Dad's self-esteem was strong. He had no problem with my mom taking charge of the household. Growing up in a household where the mother took charge was all I knew.

Whatever my father and I wanted or needed, my mom made sure we had it. She took care of all the financial expenses and made sure the bills were paid. I never heard her talk about any budgeting or financial planning. As I look back now, I wonder what in the world was she thinking. Even though she was the biggest contributor to the household, she still should have been managing what was coming in and living a little more responsible.

Money for my mom was a status symbol. She made it and spent it as quickly as she got it. All of her reckless spending was not the right message she should have been sending me and I'll tell you why. She didn't realize how closely her daughter was paying attention and what an impression she was making on my mind. I learned that money had no limits or boundaries. If you have it *flaunt* it, *spend it and have fun!*

My mother had a college education and my father was a laborer. I remember being told religiously *"You are going to college."* It was not even an option. I was going and that was that. My mother's reasoning was *"If you go to college, you can be an independent woman and take care of yourself. You will have your own money and you won't have to wind up taking care of a man."* That's when I had an *"ah ha"* moment. If I was supposed to be independent then why was she taking care of a man? She was sending me mixed messages. On one hand she was telling me *"Take care of self,* be independent and on the other hand she was literally taking care of a financially capable man.

She also told me *"Never date or marry beneath you. Always seek someone within the same socio-economic level you have achieved."* I think she subconsciously resented marrying my dad because he was not financially or educationally on her level. Maybe that's why she felt compelled to overcompensate by taking care of the family finances. It empowered her. She was able to take charge where she felt my dad was deficient. She may have even felt that he was less than a man.

Mom didn't want me to make the same mistakes she did. That's all good but parents should remember that we do grow up. At some point you have to allow your children to live their own lives. She continued to repeat the same mantra over and over "Go to college so you can take care of yourself." I believe she wanted to live life vicariously through me. She had married right after graduating from college and gotten pregnant. She never had the chance to experience life on her own and she wanted that so desperately for me.

I did graduate from high school and went on to college. During my freshmen year I met Jeff and it was love at first sight. We were inseparable. If you saw Jeff, you saw me and vice-versa. Our college years were filled with fun, especially when we both pledged joining a sorority and fraternity. In spite of the good times Jeff decided in his junior year that college was not for him. He dropped out and his family was devastated. They tried desperately to persuade him to return to college but Jeff's mind was made up. He decided that his passion was cars. He loved working on them and wanted to operate his own auto mechanic shop. We all had to finally agree that everybody is not college material. Just because you don't attend college does not make you are more or less successful than anyone else. It's all how you define what success is.

Jeff had been trying to get me to marry him for two years. Once my mom found out that Jeff was not going to graduate from college, she started the *"Drop the Jeff crusade."* He was no longer good enough for me. Remember Mama said, "Don't marry beneath you." "Marry someone on your level."

This reminds me of one my best girlfriend's mother. I think from the time she passed through her mom's uterus, her mother programmed her. She was told only to date men who were at the top of their game and pay scale. She never looked at or contemplated dating your average Joe. They didn't have a chance in hell. It was out of the question. Cora completed her college education with a degree in political science but chose a career as a flight attendant.

I thought Cora's Mom was surely going to die on the day she made that choice (*a waitress in the sky*)? Her mom was not cool with that decision. However, she did finally come to terms with it. She realized that Cora could travel, see the world and *maybe* meet a few rich perspective husbands along the way. During those years, Cora only dated men who were professionals in the corporate world, entertainers, business owners or athletes. No one else needed to apply.

Cora did hit the jackpot several times! Her mother couldn't have been happier. She met and dated corporate presidents and high profile jocks but neither of those was to be her choice. She wound up marrying an actor who shall remain nameless to protect his identity. Cora had a fairy tale wedding, a five-carat diamond ring, a new husband, and a beautiful home in Beverly Hills with all the perks. Just like the 1960's TV Show "*The Beverly Hillbillies*," She had a swimming pool, tennis court, movie theater and a powder blue Bentley convertible with powder blue rims parked ever so neatly in the driveway.

Unfortunately, when you marry for money and not necessarily for love the castle in the blue sky can come tumbling down and it did! This is the point I wanted to make. Even though her mother (*like mine*) positioned her to hob nob in all the right social circles, all the right schools and all the right men, it didn't matter because happiness is not based on these things. After three daughters later you can guess what happened to Cora...the "Big D"...divorce. She married for money and status and not for love. In spite of that her mother still saw it as a plus because she was going to get paid alimony and child support for many years. In her eyes Cora still won. That's interesting that someone would even see anything positive in a broken marriage.

Cora was in no way prepared for what was about to happen. She had been taught how to spend money and live day to day with no regard to tomorrow. Growing up she never had to work. She was given everything on a polished silver platter. Little did she know that managing money was a prerequisite to achieving financial security. In the divorce settlement she was going to get about $8,500 dollars a month. For some reason that was not enough for her because, before the end of every month Cora was short on cash. How do you go through $8,500 dollars in less than a month is beyond me? I guess when you're shopping on Rodeo Drive everyday, relaxing at the spa, and making trips to the casino it is probably very easy.

The value of a dollar meant nothing to her. She had no plan and saved nothing. So, by the time Cora's daughters turned eighteen years of age, the money train *(child support)* came to a screeching halt. She had nothing left but a designer bag. The lifestyle that she had grown accustomed to and loved was no more. She had it all and lost it. Cora was never taught how to save for a rainy day. For her it never mattered.

A career can certainly generate the finances needed to become self-sufficient and that's great. However, having some love mixed in with that equation would be an additional welcome. Jeff tried to give me that. He begged me to marry him but *"Nooo,"* I wanted the career first, just to see what it was like but that plan was soon scrapped. I found out I was pregnant in my senior year of college. That made Jeff even more determined for us to get married. When I told my mother I was pregnant, I thought the world, as I knew it was going to come to an end. There was no calming her down. When she finally did calm down, I just knew that she would choose love and marriage over a career and be happy for me. That was not to be. She didn't waste any time in letting me know that "If you marry Jeff and have this baby, I will not continue to pay for your college education." My father was in my corner but my mother wasn't hearing it. No matter what argument was proposed to her there was no reasoning. After exhausting all possibilities I made the decision not to have the baby. I never discussed this with Jeff even though he had a right to share in my decision. This is the moment when knowing how to make choices *can* and *will* affect you for the rest of your life. I realized that I had made important decisions based on pressure from others without weighing all of my options. Once you make a drastic choice like the one I did, you can't take it back.

My choice was to opt for the sedative called twilight. I wanted to be totally absent emotionally of what was about to happen. The count down began 10-9-8-7...that's as far as I could remember counting. I was consciously gone and 45 minutes later so was my baby. This was not supposed to happen to me. The plan was to finish college, marry Jeff, and have his children. All in that order. Oh, I forgot one important thing. Live the glamerous life like Cora did.

I wish my mother had been more honest with me about love. I needed to know that you can't put it on hold for some opportune time. I should have chosen love over acareer. A career would eventually happen but how often does love come along. Would've, could've or should've doesn't change a thing. Numerous philosophers and metaphysicians have informed us that cause and affect/karma are always working in the universe. It definitely did a job on me.

Back to college I went. Mom kept her word and continued to pay my tuition. Jeff...well, he never had a choice in any of the decisions that were made. That's probably why we were seeing less and less of each other. I always thought he was going to be there and that he would wait for me forever. I thought he would eventually get over the loss of our baby and me wanting to have a career. I decided when I came home for Thanksgiving break I would see him in person and try to work things out. I thought that love conquered all. Too much thinking about what I was going to do made my head hurt. To show you how much I loved him, I was willing to marry him, quit school, get a job, and whenever I could go back to school finish paying for my own tuition.

After I arrived home during Thanksgiving break, I told mom "I was going to see Jeff." Mom said, "No! You should call his mother first." My heart was pounding because I didn't know if something had happened to him. I asked her "What's going on?" and she refused to give me any information about Jeff and instead insisted that I should just call first. I didn't bother to call Jeff's mom. I hurried over to her house. Jeff's mother answered the door. I asked, "How are you? Is Jeff doing okay? Did something happen?" The words that came out of her mouth were so shocking that I can't believe I didn't faint. Jeff's mom told me that he had gotten married.

I was devastated and in disbelief. When I got home I psychologically disconnected I felt like I had lost the two things that I loved the most (*Jeff and my baby*). I was so out of it that I went to the bathroom, found a razor and went to my room with the blade in my hand. I stayed in my room for two days in darkness with the thought of the razor blade at my side cutting away all of my pain. Not one time did my mother try to console me, check to see if I needed anything or if I was dead or alive. I just found out that the man I loved was gone. I might as well have been dead. I'm sure she was probably relieved that he was out of my life and that I would meet someone more suitable to her liking.

After that, I was never the same again, nor was the relationship between me and my mom. My self-esteem hit an all-time low. I concluded that I would never experience the kind of love I shared with Jeff again. I wanted that love so much that I started buying love. When you've had no concept of financial responsibility, budgeting or the value of a dollar, what are you going to do? You're going to spend money like it grows on trees and that's exactly what I did.

I managaed to graduate from college (*I don't know how*) and landed a high paying job as a director of a government employment agency. I was making six figures and spending it as fast as I was making it. I believe I started buying the attention of men to compensate for the void and emptiness of the love I had lost. My rationale was "*If you give a man what he wants and needs, he won't leave you like Jeff did to me.*" I thought buying men things would buy me love. I put aside those beliefs that I had to be with men that were *"on my level."* That was my mothers thinking not mine. What the hell does that mean anyway when you're in love? I dropped that concept real fast and began dating men that were not of the same educational and financial background that I had been exposed to. I was dating men who were considered by some, way below the standards my mother had set in place. Why was all this so important anyway? What a man earns, his financial portfolio, educational background, how he dresses, who his parents are... do not determine what's in someone's heart or how you'll be treated. We all know that there are some men (*Let's not forget the women*) who have all these qualities and still turn out to be assholes as partners, husbands, and wives.

As I look back, I think I was also punishing myself subconciously for not choosing the life I should have had with Jeff. I had passed up what I thought was my one chance for happiness. I decided I wasn't going to live in that Cinderella make believe world that I had been led to believe. I wasn't going to fall for the (*bullshit*) I was better than that.

Money and spending meant nothing to me. I was raised that way. I became a cash cow to the men I dated. I bought jewlery, clothes, expensive dinners and little weekend getaways. It seemed like buying things for them made me feel powerful and after all money is a power substance. I loved being in control. It was an adrenaline rush for me. You can get just about anything with money, even *love I thought* but no, money can't buy you love. It certainly won't make a man stay with you if he doesn't want to.

For some reason I felt compelled to help take care of them like my mother did for my dad and me. This is how I thought it was supposed to be. Let me just interject a quick comment here. Be careful about the messages you send to your daughters and the behaviors you model. Sometimes our examples are mixed when we proclaim "Do as I say not as I do. Whether we accept it or not our children are watching and listening. I certainly was.

I began going out with a guy I worked with. I was his boss, *which was probably my first mistake.* I could hear my mom screaming and screeching in my ear "What are you doing with a man in a position beneath you and not as socioeconomically established as you?" Devin was not even a close prototype of what my mom thought a man should be. He was not financially stable, although he had some college, he came from a two-parent working family, and wasn't too bad on the eyes but she would have never approved. He was the type that had champaign taste but beer money. He was living almost paycheck to paycheck but wanted to live a lifestyle that was way above his means. Devin grew up in a household not having enough and I was brought up in one having everything.

I soon found out that we were one in the same. We both liked to spend money and I decided that he was a man after my own heart. There is one thing I know for sure. Don't marry a person that has no discipline in saving money. Somebody has to have some responsibility and neither of us seemed to know what that was. We decided to join forces anyway and get married which gave us more financial power *(that was mistake number two).* I basically took charge of how the money was to be spent I bought the house in my name because Devin's credit was bad so I foot most of the bills for lavish vacations, cars, clothes, whatever we wanted. We had two children together and they enjoyed the good life as well. We didn't have to keep up with the Joneses, we were the Joneses. Basically, I was taking care of everything but not watchin the money and checking the bank statements like I should have been *(that was mistake number three).* I soon found out that Devin's paychecks were not being deposited like I thought they were. We were spending so much that I hadn't even noticed. Now, here's the clincher.

I had planned a birthday party for my daughter at an exclusive hotel, again, I was never thinking about whether too much money was being spent or if I was being impractical. When I arrived at the hotel the day of the party the manager greeted me and asked "How would I be making the final payment?" I gave the hotel manager my credit card. When he returned with my credit card, I was informed "Your card has been declined." I couldn't believe my ears because I had $7,000.00 available credit. I never really checked because when the limit got low the credit card company just extended me more credit. The manager apologized and asked "What other form of payment would I be making?" I replied "I am going to call the credit card company to determine what the problem was." The credit card company told me my balance on the account was $62.00. They could not extend me any further credit at this time. I needed $600.00 to bring my bill up to date. I was speechless. I told the manager that I was going to the ATM to get the cash. When I got to the ATM, I punched in my code and a white receipt came out of the machine saying "denied." The party was only less than an hour away. The guests would be arriving. I didn't have any money. They didn't accept checks for a final payment and as we know most businesses don't. I knew Devin didn't have any money because he had asked me for some that morning. There was no one I could call. I would never have asked my mother. She would have lectured me on marrying someone on my level. I didn't want to hear that. There was only one thing left for me to do, cancel the party and in doing so I lost my deposit.

We moved the party to my house. I told everybody that the hotel management had informed me that there was a water leakage in the room where the party was to be and that's why we couldn't have the party there. I was totally embarrassed and angry with myself for my many irresponsbile episodes of financial mismanagement. The biggest shocker came after the party when my husband confessed to me that he was a recovering addict when he married me and that's where most of our money had gone. He had been dipping in the money jar all along. He was getting high and his friends were benefitting from his bank roll too. I guess the operative word was *recovering* and *he wasn't recovering anymore.*

After that everything went downhill like a big snowball. Here's a play by play account. A week later I found out that I was pregnant. When I told Devin, he said, "I don't want another baby!" If you have it, I'm leaving!" I thought about what he said. I didn't want to raise three kids alone so I decided to have another abortion. I never even told him. I just went ahead and did it. Weeks later he asked me about the baby. I told him there wasn't a baby anymore and that I had an abortion. As I looked into his eyes I could tell that he was high. He started screaming at me "Why did you kill my baby?" I could see he was enraged and out of control. He stormed out of the house and didn't return for days. I wasn't going to put up with this craziness so when he did return, his bags were packed by the door. I realized then that all the money that I had spent couldn't buy me love.

After the debit card and ATM incident, it was time to take a look at and review my financial assets and credit. It wasn't a pretty picture. I discovered that everything I had worked hard for was practically gone. I had been living way beyond my means. I lost the house, my car, and all my savings. You see I trusted Devin to mail all the bills once I paid them. Well, most of them never made it to the mailbox. I had no idea that the house was in foreclosure and that my car note was months behind but his habit had been well taken care of. This is the price you pay for not monitoring your finances. There was no blame game here. I could only look at myself. Life was not easy at this time since I was now homeless. I would have rather lived in a shelter than go back home to my mom's house. I didn' have much choice though, with two children. They needed some stability and I couldn't make them suffer for my choices.

Through counseling (*personal and financial*), I was able to understand how careless and irresponsbile I had been. Budgeting, saving, and investing were not words in my vocabulary. My philosophy of "*If you have it spend it*" had to change. My reckless spending and lifestyle finally came to an end. Most importantly of all, I sacrificed two precious lives that were lost in a vacuum. For them I was modeling the wrong financial behavior. They were observing me just like I had watched my mother.

I don't know if it was a self-esteem issue, a need for security, an inferiority complex, fear, or just control. How does a woman ever think that she can buy love. Well, it's happening out here in the real world and more often than one expects.

Here are just a few phrases that are expressed from various women who are paying the cost to be the boss.

➤ Where is it written that a man has to take care of a woman? A woman can spend her money any way she wants. Who is setting these standards?
➤ Men do it for women. Why can't a woman do it for her man?
➤ A woman will do whatever it takes to make her man happy... including spoiling him by any means necessary.
➤ I give him what he wants because I love him and he's good to me.
➤ Some people just like to care for others. I enjoy doing things for my man. Is that a crime?
➤ I'm just a soft hearted woman who likes to give. It's my business how I spend my money.

### Here's Some Food For Thought

When you need your car fixed, you go to a mechanic. When your drain clogs, you call a plummer, when you have legal issues you seek an attorney, and when your life is out of control you seek counseling. The main concern I had with my therapist was, why some women find the need to take care of men? Specifically me. She informed me that so many women have been there and done that. There are some that assume 90% of the financial responsibility within the relationship. My question according to her was not an uncommon one. She did indicate that there could be several possibilities why *"buying a man"* was acceptable to me. The number one reason was CONTROL. I thought about it. Maybe subconsciously I was following in my mother's footsteps. Her equation for being in charge meant *(money + power = superiority)*. She controlled everything.

This is what I observed on a daily basis. This was her idea of love and natural devotion. I watched her pamper my father to a point where he became completely dependent on her and because of that it would be almost impossible for him to leave her. She seemed to isolate him from the outside world so he would be trapped forever in her web. He had no reason to look elsewhere because he had his bread and butter right where he was. I thought this was how a woman was supposed to treat her man. I thought this was love.

The need to control a man is also an indication of fear. In the back of my mind the loss of Jeff was still a painful reality for me. I had not resolved it. I was still grieving. The men I met after Jeff, always reminded me that I could be hurt again and that maybe if I took care of them, they would not leave me. I was also fearful of not being perfect like my mother. It was definitely a fear of something. My need was to feel secure. I would choose and attract guys who liked me but had low self esteem and were insecure. Giving everything to them made me feel they belonged to me. It also made me feel that they acknowledged my competency in handling money and the relationship. Of course, this was all foolish thinking. As partners in a relationship, money should not be used as a gain for security or hold a person hostage for his/her love. You have to separate the two. Love is love. Money is money. When the man is gone, the love and the money go with him.

Since there is no such thing as a money tree there are certain money management skills that we have to teach our daughters. In fact it's never too early to learn about the value of a dollar, how to budget, and save. Today's children are facing many uncertainties in life. The economy is one. Our children are very observant and curious. They will watch what their parent's do/say and take it at face value. When we buy $200 gym shoes but can't pay their school fees then this is an indication that money is being mismanaged. We have to lead by example. The better prepared they are, they will be able to manage their own money. Remember, they will learn about money not only by what you say, but also by what you do.

*Money Doesn't Grow On Trees Even if Our Kids Believe It Does!*

➤ Collect and save pennies/coins. If you have a jar or a piggy bank, place the pennies and other coins in them. Explain to them that they should "Save to buy things you want, need, for emergencies, or for future expenses."

➤ Budgeting (Give them a reality check.) Explain that budgeting is a plan on how and what money you'll receive and how it will be spent/saved on a weekly/monthly basis. Ex: rent/mortgage, food, lights, gas, car payments/maintenance, car/life/rental/mortgage insurance, clothing, savings, pets... etc.

➤ Let them know the juice, snack cakes, and chips are not free. No one will be giving away designer jeans, shoes...or the roof that covers their little angelic heads for free. Those items cost money. When you and your friends need a ride to the mall, to a party, or anything, it takes money to ride public transportation or to put gas into a car.

➤ Summer vacations on the beach aren't cheap and remember that pet you had to have? It needs to eat and visit the veterinarian for examinations. Inform them of the importance of a budget which is not to spend more money than you make. It is to spend your money wisely. It's about priorities.

➤ Ask for help when you go to the grocery store. Find the best buy and nutritional content for your money. Read labels. Learn how to check/compare prices to make the best choices. This applies not only to grocery shopping, but also in making every day purchases. *When purchasing electronics, ask for an "Open Box." That's when an item has been previously purchased and has been returned. Customers may purchase the returned item for ½ or more off the original price.*

➤ If you give your child an allowance, start as soon as they are old enough to understand that money can buy things. Explain their allowance should be used for, (school supplies, clothing, movies...). As a child gets older, their allowance increases and so should their responsibilities. Allowances given on a monthly basis as opposed to weekly will teach your child how to budget over a longer period of time. Saving a portion of their allowance, monetary gifts, or other earnings will establish a lifelong habit of putting money aside for those special purchases or emergencies.

➢ You Want a Car. Get a Job! As children grow/mature, encourage them to find part-time jobs/work. It will teach them to manage money as well as their time.

➢ They will experience first-hand what earning a living really is. That first paycheck will be a wake-up call when they learn about taxes, contributions and deductions the government *takes* before the pay/check is in your hands or in your bank account's direct deposit.

➢ Your child should take on more responsibilities by purchasing some of their own clothing and other necessities. It will help them to appreciate how much things cost and MAYBE they will take better care of their belongings.

    ➢ If your child plans on attending college, warn her about credit card companies. They have learned that college students are excellent customers and targets. *"Buyer/Consumer Beware."* That means you mom. You may wind up being the one paying those plastic credit cards bills and debts if your child isn't able.

    ➢ Words to the Wise "Don't, I repeat, "DO NOT BUY YOUR CHILDREN whatever they ask for!" The sole purpose of budgeting is to make positive and responsible financial choices. If your *"little Susie"* is used to getting everything she wants, when she wants it, she and other "little "Susie's" will never learn, know, or understand the VALUE OF MONEY and how to prioritize.

    ➢ Teach them to say "NO" to impulse buying. It is our job to help our daughters develop responsible spending and saving habits. If we show them a balance between the two, we can preventively assist them to avoid financial difficulty and mismanagement.

**Decisions\* Decisions\* Decisions\***

At some point our daughters need to know that there are consequences for every decision made and the results of the choices can affect not only hers but others. As mothers, we tend to step in, correct or steer our children in different directions to control and or ensure a positive outcome, most times to our liking. We will try to fix things if we see that a bad choice/option is about to be made. We don't want to see them fail or suffer.

Help your daughter(s) to recognize when she's made a good vs. a poor choice/decision. Allowing them to make choices by themselves is important to their social and emotional development. However, when there is a direct threat or danger, step in and make the choice and always explain why that decision was made. As our daughter(s) grow older, there are more serious decisions to be made.

Too many times parents will focus on pushing their children to always make the right decision in hopes of saving them from making mistakes or experiencing disappointments. Sometimes it's the bad decisions that we best learn from. We must give our daughters opportunities to discover and figure things out through trial and error. As they become adults, they will need to make decisions. You won't always be available to step in and rescue them. Start preparing them now, so they'll be able to make those tough and important decisions on their own.

➤ Look/discuss the problem(s) at hand.
➤ Ask/list the things that can be done to solve the problem.
➤ Don't feed her your choices (Listen without commenting.)

Once a decision is made, ask your daughter(s) why she believes her choice was the best? What will the results be from making that choice? Determine if the plan(s) worked/failed. Always link actions to consequences. On a final note, as mothers we must always be mindful of setting good examples. If your daughters see you and others in your family making well-informed, well thought out and responsible decisions about money, they will be more inclined to make positive decisions. Remember, they are always watching and listening.

As far as what happened to Devin and me, he left the agency where we both worked and entered rehab...again. Me?

**I'm still single and waiting for another Jeff to come along!**

*five*

# Who's Afraid of the Big Bad Wolf?

"Charles seemed like a hardworking honorable man but he was a wolf in sheep's clothing. That big bad wolf stole something from
my daughter that can never be erased.
It was only by the **GRACE** of the Almighty
that I did not shoot him dead."

*Margaret Blair, 43 years old, Cleveland, Ohio*

I recently received a birthday card from my oldest daughter, Jeannie saying, "You are the *"Queen of the family."* I thought, yes, what a journey it was for me to get to this place in my life to be so wonderfully acknowledged with this title.

Growing up in the 60's and 70's was a true learning experience for my group of friends. Most of our mothers had not told us what to look for in a boyfriend or husband. We had no clue, except that he was supposed to have a job. That seemed to be all that mattered. Just make sure he was a good breadwinner. That meant he was able to support a wife and children. Since Black men were held to menial labor jobs, the community accepted any kind of employment. There was no shame in the type of job that was held.

It didn't matter if he was homely, dumb as a rock, mean, stingy, or crazy as long as he was employed.

Joining the armed services was the most successful escape for most Black men and women until the late Rev. Dr. Martin Luther King, Jr. lead a group of protesters to march against discriminatory hiring practices at companies like the Bell Telephone company. The protests forced businesses/companies to hire Blacks in white- collar jobs and positions.

I was married to one of those men that worked hard as a laborer until he became ill. He later died of cancer and I was left with two daughters. Jeannie was ten years old and Jackie was five. As the girls got older, I started thinking about dating again and possibly finding another husband. Some close friends of mine introduced me to one of their former high school friends, Charles. He sang in various popular nightclubs and with a well-known Chicago singing group.

When he wasn't performing, we would hang out at one of our four friends' homes and play cards. Bid Whist was the game. He would always make sure that I was his partner. We began seeing more and more of each other on a regular basis. We really connected and as time progressed, we became quite serious.

My family and I were members of the Catholic Church. Since I was thinking about remarrying one of the priests discussed marriage with Charles and me. We were scheduled to meet with the priest together and then separately. During the sessions I had with the priest privately, I was warned to wait a year or two before I rushed into another marriage. I believed I had enough information about Charles to take a chance after all my close friends seemed to know Charles and they thought he was a good person. They all grew up together. What could there possibly be to worry about?

I chose not to listen to the priest's advice and we were married before the year ended.

Charles had a daughter who was a year younger than Jackie. He was always bringing her over to play with my two daughters. He seemed to be a good father because he was attentive and took care of her needs. At the time I was working for the government and he worked in sales. In addition to being an entertainer, he began taking real estate classes at a nearby college. Everything seemed to be working in our favor. My life seemed so meaningless until I met Charles. He had presented himself as a hard-working, honorable, kind, charming and handsome man who made your heart skip a beat when you saw him. I began to feel that my girls and I had gotten a second chance to enjoy family life again.

After a year of marriage we produced a son. We named him Charles Jr., little Charles. We also purchased a house, which made the girls happy because they had their own rooms. They were making new friends on the block and doing well in their studies at school. Charles was settling into the home life and decided to cut down on singing and playing in the band to spend more time at home after work and school. We still both enjoyed having our friends over on the weekend's playing cards and drinking.

Several years passed and Jeannie was attending high school while Jackie was attending middle school. Charles' daughter still came over on some weekends and spent time playing with the girls. We all seemed to be doing well until one Saturday morning Charles came home from working the night shift and for some reason insisted that I go grocery shopping without him. This was unusual because we always went shopping every Saturday morning together when he got home from work, which was our routine. He told me "Take Jeannie with you and leave Jackie at the house to watch little Charles so I can get some sleep." I had never left Jackie home alone without Jeannie being with her until that day. I didn't even stop to think why he would make such a request. He said, "I'm tired." so I went to the grocery store with Jeannie. I was checking my list and adding some items to my cart when all of a sudden something so strong came over me (*mother's intuition*) telling me to stop shopping and go home as quickly as possible. Usually, I listen to my intuition and this time was no different. Always listen to your inner voice. It will never steer you wrong. I immediately left the store with groceries in the cart. I told Jeannie to get into the car. We raced home as fast as I could drive.

We ran into the house and unexpectedly to my horror Charles was standing in the hallway naked. Little Charles was standing between him and Jackie. Charles was totally shocked when he realized I was standing there. He ran into the bedroom yelling, "I'm going to sleep now!" Jackie looked very upset and scared. I immediately asked her "What was going on?" She replied, "Mommy, he tried to make me touch his thing (*penis*)!" I was totally in shock to hear her say that. No mother should ever have to hear those words coming from the mouth of her daughter about her husband/boyfriend/mate or any male relative or acquaintance. I had just witnessed the most awkward and disgusting scene between the man I married and my precious daughter. My son could see how upset his sister was so he had come to stand between the two of them attempting to protect her and keep things from going any further. He knew something was wrong but he didn't know what.

Charles had been caught off guard because he wasn't expecting me to come home so soon. His little perverted plan had failed. He had been caught in the act. It was too much for him. He ran into the bedroom to escape. I was right on his trail behind him. I demanded an account of what was going on. He had been drinking and was drunk. He passed out on the bed. I could smell the alcohol reeking from his breath and pores.

I left our bedroom quickly and immediately took Jeannie and Jackie into the kitchen. I began asking them questions about this terrible scene and whether or not they had encountered anything like this before. They both said, "This was the first time that Charles had ever tried anything like this." How was I to know if they were too scared to say anything to me, and if something like this had happened before? My daughters did inform me they had discovered a peep- hole that had been cut out behind the mirror from our bedroom into the girl's bathroom where obviously Charles could peek at them when they were bathing or refreshing themselves. At first I was furious because they knew about the hole and Charles had been watching them for who knows how long? I stormed into their bedroom to confirm what they had just stated. Charles had drilled a peephole in the wall to watch my innocent naked girls. No telling how long that hole had been there. How many months or years? I was sad to see the small hole shaved into the wall, which led into the girls' bathroom. I went back to my daughters and instructed them to "Tell me everything they could think of that Charles may have done or said to you." I also expressed to them that, "I would protect them at all costs." I reminded them that, "You are never to keep any inappropriate behavior from me no matter *who or what* it is."

I was overwhelmed with this problem but I had to deal with it. I couldn't just let it go and pretend it wasn't happening. I know a lot of women who do refuse to accept that their husbands or boyfriends have been molesting their daughters. I don't understand how they turn their heads and will not believe their daughters when they tell them. I began calling friends and family of Charles. I wanted everyone to know what he was doing. I put him on blast. I wanted to embarrass him and call him out. I also wanted to find out if his family knew about his sick behavior. I called his favorite cousin who had a daughter in Jackie's classes at school. When I told her what happened, she said, "I'm sorry about what happened to you but why is he still there? She told me that I was a good one for letting him stay. I guess I was still numb and the shock hadn't worn off yet.

Next, I called an ex-policeman who worked with Charles years ago and shared with him what happened. His advice was to "wait until he woke up to discuss this problem with him." I couldn't

believe my ears *"Wait for him to wake up."* Why? So I wouldn't inter-
rupt his sleep? I thought about it later on, why was I even calling his
police friend or his cousin. I should have called the police as soon as
I walked in the door! Why was I taking time to rationalize and think
through this horrific crime? It should have been a no brainer! I was
calling everybody but the POLICE to lock his molesting ass up!

What I should have done was cut his penis off? But then he
would have become the victim and I would have been the criminal.
Where is the justice? After Charles awoke and sobered up (*I still
can't believe I waited until he woke up.*) I confronted him on what he
had attempted to do with Jackie. Even though I caught him in the
act, he still denied doing anything wrong. When I asked him about
the hole in the girls bedroom wall to the bathroom he denied knowing anything about that. He went to the kitchen, returned with his
favorite beverage (*alcohol*), and began to drink it as if it was water.
The girls watched as he emptied the bottle. I told them "I will figure
out what to do. I won't ever leave you alone with him again." As I
continued to question Charles about what he had done, he became
more and more defensive. The confrontation with him did not go
well especially when I tried to drag him into the bedroom to see
the hole in the wall. His frustration, (*that I had uncovered his wrong
doings*) caught me off guard and he punched me in the jaw. Bam! I
fell to the floor in pain. Charles ran out of the room, came back with
a gun and shot a bullet through the dining room floor. All I could do
was hear the priest in my head telling me "Wait, don't rush into this
marriage." If only I had listened. Little Charles grabbed his ears and
the girls looked on in horror. None of us could believe what had just
happened. Somebody could have gotten shot or killed. I didn't even
know he had a gun. I was filled with fear and scared for the safety
of my children. Fortunately, Charles was so drunk he soon passed
out. This time I didn't have to think about what to do. I called the
police and had him arrested. After that episode I filed papers for a
restraining order to keep Charles away from us. Sometimes, that
piece of paper doesn't mean a damn thing. If a man or woman wants
to see you a piece of paper is not going to stop anything!

Charles pleaded with the police and anyone who would listen to him begging to see his son. Months later I did allow him to see little Charles with a police officer present. When he arrived, he fell on his knees and held little Charles in his arms crying and pleading to let him keep his son. I could see the look on the officers' faces. They actually felt sorry for him. What about the girls and me? The policeman suggested that both our lawyers needed to talk and straighten out visitation rights.

Since I had to work, I hired a babysitter to watch little Charles. One day while I was at work, I received a phone call telling me that Charles had transferred his job location to northern California and kidnapped little Charles from the babysitter. He was in the backyard playing at the time. When I found out what he had done, I asked my lawyer to have Charles served with papers to bring him back to me. It took about four months before he was returned. Charles asked for our forgiveness and said that he was in a counseling program and had also stopped drinking. My thought was that he was a desperate person who would do and say anything to regain favor and credibility. I guess I believed or wanted to believe what he was saying so I allowed him to visit little Charles and spend time with him on a regular basis. I wonder was I being gullible? Did I just want to keep my family together? Or, was it because I needed to be loved and wanted a man in my life?

As I think back, now, my first reaction was this could not be happening to me and my family. I couldn't believe the man I loved and married was a pedophile. He was manipulating my daughter and encouraging her to touch his penis. What a sick bastard! Who knows what actually happened or how frequently it happened. I felt like a bolt of lightening had hit me. I wonder to this day how much of this tragedy Jackie has blocked psychologically from her mind. At that time my survival skills kicked in and my first reaction was to kill his ass for trying to ruin my beautiful daughters' lives. I quickly regrouped and began to think about the consequences if I had killed him, I would have been sent to prison for murder and my children would have become victims of the state system. That's the only thing that kept me together.

My mind began to wander back to a childhood incident that happened to one of my friends when I was twelve years old. I was sitting with a group of girls sitting on a bench in our courtyard during a summer evening. We were talking and laughing like preteens do. One of the girls, Marlene, was just thirteen years old and every Thursday evening like clockwork, her mother, Mollie would dress up in high heels and tip out to the neighborhood beer garden leaving Marlene and her younger brother at home with their stepfather. After Marlene's Mom, Mollie left the house and the streetlights came on, Marlene's stepfather would call out to Marlene and tell her "It's time to come in. Marlene would always ignore him as long as possible before shouting back, "What do you want? Of course he would remind her "It's dark. Time to come in." Back then you had to be in the house when the streetlights came on. Some of you may remember those days. The other girls and I would ask her "Why are you talking to your stepfather so mean?" Marlene responded, "He makes me sick!" We couldn't believe how she talked to him because it was unheard of. When an adult told you to do something, you just did it. No questions asked and certainly no talking back (*not like today*).

After summer was over, we all went back to school. During the winter months most of us stayed indoors unless we came out to make snowmen or angels in the snow. Just before Easter, we noticed Marlene had gained a lot of weight around her belly area. To our surprise, she told us she was going to have a baby soon. We all assumed the father was a young boy down the hill who she played around with at times. We didn't give it a second thought until the baby was born. Then all the gossip began. Marlene had a healthy baby boy who came out looking exactly like her stepfather. At least that's what everybody said. The baby looked nothing like the boyfriend down the hill who we thought was the daddy. Marlene's mother, Mollie brought the baby outside to show him off several months later and said, "This baby is mine". None of us knew what to say. I stood up and said, "We already know the baby is Marlene's! She told us it was hers. You ain't fooling us!" We were all shocked that she would try to pass off the baby as hers. How stupid did she think people were?

Mollie was so proud as she showed all of us the newborn baby boy. She kept commenting on his features (the color of his skin) and his hair. She seemed to be more concerned that the baby was light-skinned with curly brown hair. During that time a lot of Black people believed that the lighter your skin was and the texture of your hair were a major factor in determining if a baby was pretty or not. Mollie seemed more concerned about that and less concerned about her then fourteen-year old daughter having a baby by her husband. All I could think about was this same thing could have happened to Jackie.

Returning to my problem, I decided to call as many friends and relatives as I could think of to get some perspective of what I should do. No one wanted to talk openly about what had happened. These kinds of situations have always been *hush-hush*. No one talked about rape/sex abuse, especially, if it happened in the immediate family. It was never talked about or addressed by my mother. This really helped me to see the need for this topic to be discussed more openly. We have to talk about it. It cannot be buried or ignored.

After Charles' father and family members were informed of what Charles had attempted to do to my daughter (*I mean I told everyone but the news media network.*), Charles and I separated and I filed legal documents to get custody of our son. During this time apart, Charles demonstrated a sincere concern to be with his son and do better as a husband and father. He later apologized to my daughters and me for behaving so badly. It didn't matter what he said because I would never trust Charles around my daughters again.

We both called on the church and with their support and coun-seling we slowly became a *"family"* again. Why did I stay with him? That is a million-dollar question. I think I wanted a man in my life (*at what cost?*) and I remember the priest saying, "You have to for-give and move on with your life." Even with that being said things were still different for all of us. The respect for him was gone and married life as we knew it would never be the same again. I was stronger now and I started taking charge and making decisions about important matters. I felt like he had lost his privileges of being the man of the house. Basically, he was just like a tenant living in the house. He became invisible to the girls and me. How could he lead us after what he had done?

I learned that you can't depend on others to make you happy. And, *A MAN* damn sure can't make you happy and that's what I thought he was going to do. Don't look to a man or anyone to bring you happiness. You have to be happy with yourself first. You can't expect them to be the person you think they should be or what you want them to be. Another reason why I stayed was for my son. He loved his father very much and wanted to be with him so I guess at that time I figured it was better than having no man in his life at all. I know that may sound crazy but that was a decision I had to make, good bad or indifferent. I did make certain he had positive males in his life from church, his coaches, and people in education that demonstrated the qualities needed to be a good man. My daughters left the house as soon as they were able (*I can't blame them for that*). They both have successful careers in education and are still single.

### Beware of the Predator

Here are some thoughts about pedophiles...it doesn't matter if their sexual fantasies are just a thought in their minds or if they have intentionally carried out the act. The crime has still been commit-ted. The Internet is a major outlet/source for sex offenders/solici-tors (*to act out their sexual behaviors*) to obtain/recruit minors. If at all possible keep the computer in a room where *you* can supervise your child's activities.

Young girls may think it's exciting to meet guys on various media sites. There's nothing like an older guy filling your head with compliments and making you feel older. This is the age of technology and social media where participating in negative behaviors seems to be the norm. Let them know that there are some people on these sites that lie about who they really are and what they are really like in order to meet youngsters and teens for sexual encounters. It doesn't matter how or where...a pedophile is a pedophile! It is what it is! It's physical, mental, emotional and spiritual abuse. We CANNOT justify, accept or tolerate this behavior. It is easy to fall for their *Internet flattery and* charm. Explain to them how dangerous this can be and discourage them from meeting people and sending personal photos and information to people they don't know. Tell them to never give their real names, addresses, or phone numbers on any on-line sites where they can be traced.

Instead of the *"old school silent treatment "Don't kiss or tell."* that I got from my mother about sex, I decided it was important to not only talk about sex but to inform them early about the sacredness and privacy of their bodies. I told them to "Always alert me when you feel you are in danger of anything and be aware of your surroundings." I had to remind myself that they are just children. They are not thinking about those kinds of things but we must continue to make them aware. You cannot count on them solely to be able to alert you when something happens. Their minds are on playing with their dolls or going to the movies. That is why it is our responsibility as mothers to protect them as best we can.

**What to tell your daughters about sexual abuse:**

➢ Talk openly with your daughter(s) about sexual development. Use appropriate and medical terms for body parts (penis and vagina).

➢ Tell them if anyone attempts, tries or touches their private parts, or encourages them to touch or look at another person's private parts, talks to them about sex, constantly walks in on them while in the bathroom or does anything to them that makes them feel uncomfortable, they are to tell you immediately. Check your daughter(s) closets, bedroom walls, and bathroom walls for any signs of holes, where someone could observe them.

➢ Inform them that they don't have to keep secrets. Comfort them and let them know that you are here to protect them.

➢ Tell them that some people will try to trick them into keeping secrets by offering candy, money, trips, clothing, threaten to harm/hurt you, or other family members, punish you, or take you from your family. Inform them to ignore the threats and still tell your parents or a responsible adult EVERYTHING. We want the TRUTH!

➢ Tell them you will not be mad with them if they tell you when someone has touched them inappropriately. Inform them that, "It's not your fault."

➢ Keep a list of people they can call on for support or help if for some reason you are not available. Put their phone numbers in a location that is accessible to them.

➢ It's okay to say "No" to someone older than you or people in authoritative positions if they are being told to do something that makes them feel uncomfortable.

I don't know if your mother did this to you but mine sure did. She would make me hug and kiss Uncle Robert when he would come to visit us. Now, that I think about it, he would hold and kiss me just a little bit too long. I would always say to her, "I don't want to kiss him. I hate it." Never force your daughter to kiss or hug other people when they don't want to especially men.

Sometimes children will not tell you right out that they have been sexually abused. The best practice would be to read between the lines. The warning signs are there. If your daughter(s) are telling you things like *"I don't like the babysitter"*, I don't want to spend the night with a particular relative or becomes upset when that person is around them, ask them about it and assure them that you will not allow them to be in that persons company. If they begin using sexually explicit language, this could be a warning sign as well.

When choosing a day care center or camp always ask, "If they do criminal background checks on their volunteers and employees." Make certain you find out if the children are ever left alone with adults, especially, during the times they take naps or go to the washroom. If your daughter(s) tell you that they have been abused believe it. There are so many parents that refuse to believe their child. It may be difficult to believe that an adult or older child has committed such an act, but accepting that it did happen can aid in the recovery of the child. Allow your child to be as factual as possible about the abuse. Again, let them know right away "It is not their fault. The abuser is to blame." Always report the abuser to your local police department immediately. If you need further support or assistance you can contact the sexual abuse hotline at 1(800) 422-4453.

Don't make this a one- time conversation. Communicate with your daughter(s) on a daily basis. Ask her questions about her day and the people she encountered or interacted with. Periodically play *"what if"* games. Provide various scenarios/situations. Discuss with her how she would handle the situation if she were faced with a crisis. Look at several other options that would help to resolve the problem.

**Inform and Protect Our Daughters!**

# six

# It's a Thin Line Between Sanity

# and Madness

"I was only ten years old when I started hearing
voices and seeing shadows of men I didn't know.
I realized I had passed the point of no return
and reality, as I once knew it, no longer existed.
My life became a living nightmare. For the next
twenty five years… I was a tortured soul."

*Rafia Ismail, 49 years old, Newark, New Jersey*

Racism and psychotic episodes would haunt me most of my life
but you would never know that by looking at me. I came from a
middle class two-parent family in the late 1970's. Of course that's
when there was a middle class status. My parents were hard working and my brother and I attended the best schools. At a young age
he was shipped off to a military school because my mother thought
that was prestigious and she wanted to be part of the movers and
shakers. We lived in the most affluent neighborhoods and we were
dressed like the mannequins you see in the best upscale department
stores. We were the *model family* living *the American dream*. We
had the two- car garage and the white picket fence. But, beneath the

exterior and outer appearance there was one tortured soul. I was battling with evil demons inside of me.

I want to take you back to the beginning, where my nightmare began. I wasn't really schooled on the subject of sex until I was molested at eight years old. I grew up in the early 1970's where most of the girls my age were still playing with dolls, jumping rope, playing hop scotch and hide and go seek. *Sex* back then was reserved for marriage or least that's what we were taught. You didn't even consider having sex until then. Being a virgin was more the norm rather than the exception. Sex education in the schools did exist but it was limited. At home discussion of sex was taught as the *"birds and the bees."* It was a means of indirectly explaining to a child the basic information about sex, where babies originated in a roundabout way by explaining through *nature's* point of view. The debate over who should be responsible for telling their children about sex is still an ongoing issue. With high numbers of teenage pregnancies and sexually transmitted diseases sex education needs to be an essential part of a child's learning regardless of who addresses it. I grew up in a strict household where sex was not a topic of discussion. Good touch or bad touch was never discussed. That was not a term that was used while I was growing up.

My mother was a teacher and claimed to be a humanitarian. She would take in families down on their luck. She especially favored taking in college and foreign exchange students who would come live with us during the school session. She enjoyed her status in our community and socializing with her colleagues after work and sometimes on the weekends. She was a functional alcoholic that worked out to her advantage. She could work all day and engage in her favorite activity...drinking all night. I used to beg her on the evenings she chose not to go out. I told her that I didn't want to be left with the babysitter because I knew what was going to happen.

At the time we had a single mother and her son, Phillip, who was about fourteen years old living with us, but he looked much older because he was so big. Since she was always playing social services with the needy she moved them right into our home. Dad never had too much to say and he always let my mother have her way. I don't know what spell she had over him but it worked! My mother felt this was extremely convenient for her. When she would go out she would give Phillip authority to take care of my brother and me. He was the official built in babysitter. His mother worked nights and was rarely there. My father who worked two jobs was not there either so Phillip was in charge.

As soon as I heard the front door close, I knew what was about to happen. Before Phillip came looking for me, I would always hide my brother in a safe place and told him "Don't come out until I come get you." I was always fearful that he might hurt or molest my brother too. I can't remember exactly how many times I was sexually assaulted. I guess I blocked it out. Once I felt that sticky wet liquid running between my legs (*I had no clue what that was*) he made me get up and immediately dragged me to the front closet and locked me in. I would always remain there until just about the time he thought my mother would be coming home. He would repeatedly tell me that, "You are bad and bad girls have to be punished!" (*I never figured out nor did he tell me why I was bad*).

Phillip told me several times that "If you ever mention this to anyone, especially your mother or father, I will kill your entire family." (*My brother would hear his threats so he didn't want to say anything either*). Of course I believed him so, I stayed in the dark closet crying and believing that I was a bad girl. After all Phillip said I was! To this day my brother and I have never talked about what happened on those nights. I never asked him if Phillip ever touched or molested him either. I guess it will always remain the unspoken word between the two of us, even now as adults.

I knew in my heart, even as a child what Phillip was doing was wrong. Your instinct or inner voice will always tell you when something isn't right. You must always listen. I decided after months of this injustice to my secret garden that I would take a chance and tell my mother what was happening to me. To my surprise she didn't believe a word I told her. Her response was "Girl, go play. Why would you make up something like that? You know that boy didn't do anything to you." I begged her "Please just come home early one night and see that I'm not lying." Regardless, of what your daughter may tell you, I don't care what it is, always listen to them. Whether you believe them or not at least investigate.

The attacks went on for what seemed like years. It's hard to figure how much time has actually passed when you're a child. I carried this fear with me until we finally moved to another location of the city (*my mother was always looking for a bigger home in a more upscale neighborhood*). This time it was to my advantage because Phillip and his mother had to find another place to live. They were not going with us. His mother had saved up enough money to get their own place. I think this was one of the happiest days of my young life. The day they left, Phillip never said a word to my brother or to me but the look he gave me was ingrained in my mind for a long time. I often wondered if there were other girls that he subjected to his sexual appetite. Somehow, I think there were. The molestation stopped but the damage had already been done. From that moment on my life became a living nightmare.

As I grew older, I would find solace in talking to my mother's older sister, Elaine. She had been through some of the same things that I had experienced. A family member molested her at an early age and that was one of her problems. She also had a difficult time being accepted by whites and blacks because she was very fair skinned and I was too. In fact, she could have passed for White if she had wanted to. The Whites would harass her because she was Black and the Blacks would ostracize her because she wasn't Black enough. As close as we were I was able to talk to her about the racism that both of us experienced but I still could not find it within myself to tell her about the molestation. I thought maybe she wouldn't believe me either. I guess it was just too painful and I continued to bury it further inside of me.

Aunt Elaine tried to tell me why my mother acted the way she did. She explained to me that her skin color (*She was just as light complexioned as my aunt*) and the fact that she was the only one in the family to graduate from college she believed she was better than everybody else. When you have this attitude, you feel like you are privileged and everyone should be held to a higher standard allowing little room for error. My aunt said, "Your mom acts that way to hide behind the terrible secrets that she experienced in her childhood." I soon discovered from our conversations that my grandmother, aunt, mother, and I all belonged to a generational cycle of tortured souls. We had all been molested!

I made a vow that if I gave birth to daughters, this would never happen to them. I knew in my heart that this pain would stop with me. No more tortured souls! I made a promise to myself that I would always listen to what they had to say and keep the lines of communication open to them. I would talk to them about good touch bad touch and the evil pitfalls of racism.

I was fourteen years old when the voices started. Soon after that came the visions. I would hear audible voices or words that I couldn't understand. Sometimes, if I listened closely it sounded like they were calling my name. I would see things like shadowy figures of men in dark coats and hats. I was a scared and confused girl. When I told my mother what I was experiencing she said, "Oh that's just the devil talking to you." Of course that didn't settle my fears and once again my mother dismissed my deep concerns.

Eventually, she could see that there was something terribly wrong and finally sought counseling and psycho-therapy for me. This was a very difficult time for me as a child or for any child to grasp and understand the ramifications of molestation and how it affects one's life. I was diagnosed with schizoaffective disorder. I was told that this was a serious mental illness that affects the brain and mood. The doctor explained to me that, sexual abuse or any kind of negative abuse can permanently affect the physical development of a child's brain. These physical changes can result in psychological and emotional problems that may exist well into adulthood". Some of the symptoms include hallucinations, delusions, and disorganized thinking. It's estimated about one in every 200 people or (0.5%) develops schizoaffective disorder at some time during his or her life. I tried to bury those demons deep into my subconscious but it did not work. Several medications were prescribed for me to stabilize my mood and treat the psychotic episodes. At that time I didn't realize that the mind is a very powerful piece of equipment.

During the rest of my adolescent years something inside of me died and I started to withdraw from people. Hearing voices and seeing things didn't make it easy for me to blend in with the other kids and I wasn't living a normal life. Unfortunately, the story does not end here. You would think that this was enough to deal with but there was still more. There was yet another truth for me handle... RACISM.

Since I was older my father shared some startling news with me that was shocking. He said, "When you were born, I swore that you were not my daughter. I believed your mother had an affair and had gotten pregnant by another man. You didn't look anything like me. You arrived in this world with red hair, white skin, freckles, and blue eyes." I could certainly understand his reservations. Even though both my parents had lighter complexions they were still African American. With my mother's persistence, he eventually was convinced that I was his child. Even so, that did not take away what I had to endure.

According to the old adage *"I was light damn near white."* That meant I was a very light complexioned Black girl. I tried hard to make friends during my high school and college years. I never seemed to fit in anywhere, not with Blacks or Whites. I was taunted, teased and called all kinds of names. I wanted to belong so badly (*to a group*). I just knew that as I got older, racism would just disappear. It didn't register that when I went away to attend college, the slate would *NOT* be wiped clean. I didn't think *RACISM* existed in the adult world I thought people would be more understanding the older you got. I was surprised. It got worse. How naïve I was to think it was only a child's game. I soon realized that it was indoctrinated in the fabric of our entire society.

I remember trying out for the Miss Black University Pageant. What a big mistake that was! I was totally insulted and humiliated in front of my own peers. I still can't believe that the student committee said that, *"I didn't look Black enough."* They all sat there and laughed at me. My showing up to enter the contest made me the biggest joke on campus. I was told to go tryout for the White campus queen pageant instead. They told me to enter that contest and that I would have a better chance. You see racism is not always about white people despising or hating on Black people. RACISM is racial differences in character and intelligence...that asserts the superiority of one race over another race. All I could do was run out the door. At this point I stopped hanging out with everyone who claimed to be my friend but wasn't. After that I never stated my *true* ethnic identity to anyone again. If someone asked me, I would let them guess and whatever answer they gave, that's who I became.

It seemed like the guys on campus tended to be more accepting of me than the women. In my mind I believed that the dark skin guys wanted me because I looked white. They wanted to be with me because they couldn't get a white girl. I was the closest and next best thing to it. See how deep and twisted racial roots can grow?

All of these events affected my psyche and I made a conscious decision to never date or marry a dark skinned man. Why? Because all the hurt I experienced in my short life-time was a result of what Black men had said or done to me. That included Phillip my molester who was dark skinned too. The experiences I had in college with dark skin men proved to be disenchanting. I knew they only wanted me because of the color of my skin. They had no idea of who I was, what I was about or what a good person I really was.

In this society *"White means privileged."* It seems your stock goes up the whiter you look. The forces in control are the ones who determine *"What is and who is beautiful."* And, they determine *"who's in and who's out"*. In this country and some of the others, *(and you can say what you want)* but there is a definite social stigma attached to darker skin. The Black men I met associated with me because the color of my skin was closer to the American dream of *white is right.* I was just a showpiece to them.

After college I met a wonderful man. No, he was not African American. He was from the Middle East. Remember, I said that I would never date or marry anyone from my own race. I was turned off totally. My family was never accepting of him but that didn't matter to me. It seemed as though he was the only man that understood and accepted me for who I was. There was no issue with him about my color, my emotional state or anything about my past. His family did not care about my color or racial identity either. I could talk to him about all of my secrets. I didn't feel like I was being judged. We did eventually get married but before that took place, I accepted Islam, and by the grace of Allah I finally started to get some mental and emotional healing. Everyone has their own solution or ways for handling their problems. There are many avenues and roads to do that. I always knew there was a higher power in the Universe and for me that was Allah. I started to see a glimmer of light through the dark tunnel I had become a captive to. My tortured soul still has a ways to go and the voices and visions are still my constant companions but not as much.

I continued to seek psychiatric help. I needed to be well informed and become a *whole* woman as much as possible for my daughters. I stayed in therapy for approximately 25 years. I have lived most of my life in therapy sessions and off and on prescribed medications. Even though I have discontinued the meds, I still see a therapist from time to time. My battle with deep depression and schizophrenia has basically run its course. The teachings of Islam, an exceptional husband, and a good therapist have been beneficial in my healing process. I thank Allah every day for guiding and allowing me to understand that the sexual abuse was not my fault. It was out of my control. As far as the evils of racism are concerned it will not change the color of my skin. I have to love me for who I am.

Even though my daughters are adults now and living their lives, I have always been available to them to talk about men, racism, sex, and life in general and we continue to do so. There is an open line of communication between us. They know they can talk to me freely about anything. No subject is off limits. The risk of my daughters developing a mental illness was a real concern to me because it can be inherited through the genes. Two of my four daughters were affected. One was diagnosed as bi-polar. The other one has severe depression. They were both teens when I recognized the symptoms. I encouraged them to get help in spite of their reservations. They didn't want to be labeled or teased by other kids while growing up. They did get counseling and the proper medication allowing them to live a normal life. As adults they still have minimal bouts with their personal issues but it is manageable and they are living productive lives.

It is unconscionable that our society still remains in the dark ages. We don't have to hide or lock ourselves in a room because our brain is sick. If you have symptoms of a migraine headache, would you continue to stay in pain? (*probably not*). You would seek professional help from a specialist to get some relief. Well, this is the same thing. If you are emotionally ill, you will get professional help for that. We are very sensitive toward people with cancer or any other disease but for some reason mental illness is almost insignificant. We are labeled as crazy, ready for the nut house, or need to see a shrink. Comedians make jokes about mental illness and it is further reinforced in movies, television and other media outlets as entertainment. Unfortunately there is nothing funny about mental illness.

Telling my daughters my story and sharing it with you will hopefully open a dialogue with others about the importance of mental health. Talking to your daughter (s) about mental illness can provide an opportunity to share factual information with support and guidance about healthy mental living. Communicate with them. They need to know that if something is bothering or worrying them (e.g. loss of appetite, feeling angry all the time, can't sleep, difficulties concentrating, or feelings of nervousness), they should ask questions. Knowledge is power. The truth is the light. Share your life experiences with your daughter(s).

I would like to express this sentiment to you. "Always be true to yourself, love yourself, and your Creator."

Love Peace Happiness!

### When Mom Doesn't Feel Well Tell Her

➢ They are not to blame for their parent(s) illness. They are not the cause of it.
➢ Just because your parent has a mental illness, doesn't mean you will. You can't catch it like a disease.
➢ Reassure them that you are getting medical assistance to resolve your problems.
➢ Help them to formulate the best explanation of their illness to their family/friends, if they should ask.

Explain to them that "Sometimes people can and will say mean things about people with mental illness."

➢ Give her an opportunity to discuss how she feels. Allow her to ask questions. Address her concerns.
➢ Remember to always use language and explanations that are age and intelligence appropriate.

**What's Good What's Bad? Good touch vs. Bad Touch**

- ➤ A good night hug/kiss feels good from mom, dad or other family members. This can be demonstrated by showing how someone should kiss, hug or touch them.
- ➤ Let them know "a good touch" makes one feel happy safe and loved. Demonstrate what "a good touch"
- ➤ A bad touch is when someone touches you in the breast/chest area, vagina, lower posterior/buttocks, or any private parts of the body, inform the person(s) firmly and harshly "Off limits!" Your body belongs to you and no one else. Say "No" to a person if you don't like the touch. RUN! AVOID staying alone with the person(s). Tell an adult or person you TRUST and know that s/he will do something to assist you. Tell your parent(s), a teacher, a relative... and if they don't believe you FIND someone else to help you.
- ➤ A bad touch makes one feel scared, nervous or uncomfortable.
- ➤ The person threatens to hurt you or a family member if you tell someone. (DO NOT KEEP SECRETS! TELL someone!)

Never blame yourself. You did nothing wrong. Don't allow anyone to blame you.

**Superior vs. Inferior**

**I don't think I'll ever see the end of racism in my lifetime. We are all from the Human Race So....... ERASE RACISM.... This Joke Is A Prime Example!**

**Racism** is when you run over a nigger with your truck.

**Reverse racism** is when you back the truck up!

Racism is alive and well. This joke was meant to be funny but *for whom* and to *what expense*? Starting a conversation about race is not an easy task, especially with younger children. We must prepare our daughter(s) for the ugliness of racism and sexism. Whether you have experienced it or not, it is alive and well. Not talking about it will not make it go away.

Teaching your daughter(s) about different races/cultures/ skin colors will help them to understand we are all different. Treat everyone the way you want to be treated.

> Be a role model. Teach by example. If they see you speak out against racist comments/attitudes or witness racist behaviors, they will learn to speak out against it too.
> Purchase books or obtain documentaries for your daughter detailing the lives of historical figures that have fought against racism. Discuss them with her.
> Encourage them to make friends from other races and different backgrounds.

Children will easily imitate, mimic and repeat what they see, do and hear. If you observe your child participating in racist acts, behaviors or associates with children who practice these unacceptable behaviors, CORRECT IT IMMEDIATELY! Don't believe they will grow out of it. Nothing is cute about racism. It is no joking matter.

"Why shouldn't white people go swimming? "

"Because crackers get soggy when wet."

What is the point of Jewish football?

To get to the quarterback

*START THE DIALOGUE

***NOW***

*seven*

# Deadly Craving for Love

"I thought I had married my prince charming, the man of my dreams. I was on cloud nine and nothing else in life mattered until the day he put a knife to my throat. I was obsessed with a deadly craving for love."

*Sharon Greene, 56 years old, Washington, D.C.*

It had been many years since I had seen Matthew. In fact we had not seen each other since college. He saw me first and called out my name. When I turned around I was pleasantly surprised to see this handsome man. He had not changed much and he was even better looking than what I had remembered him to be in college. We were quite an item on campus. He embraced me with a hug and we talked briefly about our past and the good ole days. While we were dating things weren't always as they should have been between us but we were trying to work on the relationship. What we needed was a break to see if we really wanted to be together and if we wanted to work things out. It was a good thing and a bad thing that the government stepped in and took Matthew away from me, just like the late Dr. Seuss' children story, *"The Grinch Who Stole Christmas."* I didn't want him to go to war but the decision was not his. Whoever said,

95

"All is fair in love and war" was a liar. I couldn't see the significance of anyone's life wasted in some hotter than hell jungle fighting and killing a race of people who like us have experienced nothing but a history of hatred and racism. What had they done to us?

Even though Matthew was off to fight a war for his country, we had already experienced our own personal war while we dated in college. As most stories begin, everything was just fine between us. Matthew was attentive and romantic. We always had fun hanging out with family and friends. As the months of our dating went by I noticed a change in him. The once romantic relationship turned into an unhealthy and violent hell.

Matthew attempted to change me in*to what he wanted me to be.* He was choosing what clothes he wanted me to wear and the people I hung out with. He didn't want me to associate or social-ize with my friends and family anymore. If anything went wrong or didn't go well in his life, he would blame me. Matthew became possessive, controlling, physical and violent. I had to account for every minute of my days and nights to Matthew with *no exception.* If I didn't answer the phone when he called or met him at a certain time that he designated, I became a victim to his uncontrollable temper. I no longer had a life, friends or family. I was no longer able to participate in any of my extracurricular activities at school.

I remember talking to a male classmate about an assignment at the library. Matthew saw me talking to him and later, when we were alone he accused me of cheating on him and said, "You are making a fool out of me in front of my friends." I paid for that conversa-tion with bruises to my face and scratches on my body. There was no disagreeing with him. Any little thing I did that didn't meet his approval would spark his anger.

I know my mother had to have seen the bruises on my body. Heck, they were accumulating. She never said a word to me about them. She believed Matthew was the perfect gentleman from a good family. That's all that mattered to her. In her eyes "It was just a little lovers' quarrel." I wanted to escape this abusive relationship but I couldn't. I was filled with fear and shame. I couldn't face my friends or family with the reality of my relationship. I did my best to explain his behavior and protect him and myself from being exposed to the truth of what was really happening. I always minimized his temper tantrums and made excuses for his extreme behavior. In time and in my mind I kept thinking that things between us would change and get better (*what inside our head makes us believe this?*). Unfortunately, most times that didn't occur. Matthew was an extremely good-looking guy. I was drawn to his physical attributes and intellect. I really wanted to be with him so much that I sacrificed my own self-respect. I would have rather been with him than without him. I didn't think I could ever get anyone like him again.

In spite of everything that happened between us it was really good to see him again and especially to know that he had survived the war. I had put the war we experienced behind us too and chalked it up as being a part of growing up (*like my mama said*). Matthew suggested that we get together again soon and that maybe we could continue where we left off (A 100 watt light bulb should have turned on in my head). If you experienced dating abuse on the front end, isn't it possible that you might experience it on the back end?

We exchanged numbers and promised each other that we would see each other soon. A week later we were doing just that. We had a romantic dinner but during our conversation I could tell that he had seen the ugliness of war. I instinctively knew the war had changed him. This is where I should have made my exit...stage left, but I didn't. I somehow managed to dismiss the pain and abuse that I had experienced with Matthew in the past and swept it under the rug. I figured we were mature adults now and the kiddie love was behind us.

It's funny how when you're dating, one fails to find or see a man's faults and short-comings and vice-versa for a woman. I had observed on many occasions Matthew's nervousness. He was always fidgeting and jittery and he experienced bouts of paranoia. I always dismissed it as P.T.S.D. (*Post Traumatic Stress Disorder*). I figured he would seek counseling for that. Why didn't I confront Matthew about his behavior? Why didn't I ask questions? Why didn't I ask him about all the dark marks that I saw on his body? It didn't matter because in the long run the answers would be revealed and they wouldn't be pretty.

It was 2:00 p.m. on a beautiful sunny day. I was glad that I had taken the T- tops off my sports car. The sky was unusually bluer than normal. The warm sun kissed my skin while the lightly cool breeze let me know that God was blessing me today. I only had a few more errands to run before 5:00 p.m. I needed to hurry after all, this was the biggest day of my life...my wedding. Oh, I didn't tell you. Matthew asked me to marry him. I said, "Yes!" Anyway, wouldn't you know it, of all days there would be so much traffic. I only had one more stop to make and then I could go home and relax until I became Matthew's bride.

I was slowing down for a pedestrian walking across the street when all of a sudden I heard someone's car brakes screeching and then a loud crash. Suddenly, I felt faint and dizzy as if I might have passed out. It was quite an accident. A car had hit me on the driver's side. Glass was everywhere. It looked as though the car had been put through a paper shredder. An Accident? How could this be on the happiest day of my life? This was probably an omen but I wasn't listening. I should have gone immediately to the hospital. There was shattered glass all over me. I could feel the cuts and scratches on my face and body. It didn't even occur to me that I could be hurt. All I could think about was getting married to Matthew.

Once the police report was filed I went home sore and disoriented. Somehow, I pulled myself together and made it to the church on time. The wedding was perfect but the best part was hearing the minister say, "I now pronounce you, husband and wife." I finally had the man of my dreams...

Sometimes, we get so blinded by how good looking a man is, or get so caught up in having a man that we don't take the time to get to know or see him for who and what he really is. We get a CRAVING for love at any cost. In the end that may not be in our best interest and it could even be deadly. We need to scratch a little bit more below the surface. Look a little deeper. We need to see the signs *(that are flashing like neon lights)*, and even if you don't see anything, look for them anyway. Don't just ignore them or think that the signs will go away. When they say something crazy, listen carefully. Most times that doesn't happen because we really don't want to know. We ignore all the warning signs. These are the areas where we fall short. This is a mama's lesson to teach our daughters for sure.

Beauty is only skin deep. There is more to a person other than his/her outer shell. You need to look at who a person is and what s/he stands for. Don't get me wrong, physical looks are good but they are superficial. Being with someone because s/he is attractive is shallow. The important thing is what they bring to the table, to the relationship and how s/he is going to treat you *(physically, mentally financially and emotionally)*. Ask questions about their family, past history, future career goals, health related issues, and extra-curricular activities for starters.

We had only been married for a month when on this particular morning I had overslept. I jumped out of bed, yelled to Matthew "Hurry up! Get out the bathroom! I'm late for work!" I waited several minutes for a response. There was none. I went to the door and asked, "What are you doing in there? Still, there was no answer. I turned the door handle. The door was locked. I couldn't understand why until I picked the lock and swung open the door. It was the most shocking sight that my eyes I had ever seen. Matthew was sitting on the floor slumped over the toilet. A sudden coldness swept over my body. Was he sick? Had he passed out? Did I need to call the ambulance? As I walked closer to him I could see that the medics or ambulance wouldn't be necessary. He was just nodding. The needle was securely stuck in his arm. A spoon, matches, and an empty plastic sandwich bag lined with white residue were still lying on the floor close beside him. I froze. I was totally numb. I would not have been able to move if my life had depended on it. It was as if I were watching a movie. Unfortunately, I had the starring role, and my leading man was a bonafide JUNKIE! Some people say you live your heaven and hell right here on earth. If that is true, hell is where Matthew took me equipped with the fire and brimstone. Matthew's primary focus in life became finding money for drugs like a hungry dog searching for scraps of food anywhere he could find it. All of his time was spent getting high and riding his thoroughbred white horse (*heroin*).

We received so many gifts from our wedding that we had to store them in our guest bedroom. It's funny. As I look back on it, I never noticed how all those gifts started disappearing one by one. It took less than a month to clear out the spare bedroom. Day by day, little by little, our wedding gifts slowly disappeared into the arms of his other woman. He sold EVEYTHING we had! When all the gifts were gone he began selling my personal belongings as well. Words to the wise, don't ever try to compete with Lady Heroin... you'll never win. No matter how hard I tried to get him back, the more she dug her heels into him.

The phone rang late one night. It was 3:00 am. I answered "Hello. ...Matthew, where are you? Oh you're in jail, for what this time? You did what?" This fool had put metal washers in coin wrappers and put a quarter at each end and tried to sell rolls of them at a currency exchange? They decided to open one of them and found out there was no money in it except one real coin at the end of each roll. "No, I can't come bail you out. I have no money to spare." Most of our money was spent going into his weakened veins.

When you're married to an addict you live in constant fear of the next phone call, informing you the person you love is either in jail or dead. You also have to think about your own safety from him and his drug buddies hanging out at your house. I lived my life as if I was stuck in a bad dream. I never knew what state of mind he was in. I didn't want to say anything or do anything to upset him because his frequent bouts of violent behaviors were causing me to constantly fear for my life. Anyone who has ever lived with an addict knows that they would kill his/her own mother or father for a fix let alone a spouse or partner.

One night Matthew came home and stated, "I have had enough of the drug scene. I want to stop." We had been in counseling with a social worker and that didn't help much. Matthew wasn't strong enough to stay clean. Out of nowhere he expressed to me that he was going to go cold turkey. I'll just stop using it and that's exactly what he did. One night he went into the bedroom and made me promise that I would not come in. I did promise and locked the door behind him. It was two days later and my curiosity had gotten the best of me. The bedroom was quiet now. The screams of pain and horror seemed to be over. I couldn't imagine what was going on in there or what it looked like with the hours of agony that had taken place So, I unlocked the door and opened it slowly. It was a sight to see, as I peeked through our bedroom door. The smell of vomit and human waste filled my nostrils. As I glanced around the room, it was in disarray. Lamps were turned over. Curtains had been pulled down from the windows. I saw Matthew sleeping like a newborn baby so I slowly closed the door and prayed that he would never have to cold turkey again. Unfortunately, that was not to be.

Weeks thereafter, I would find hidden needles, cooking spoons and white powder in places that you wouldn't believe (under the carpet, in vases, in books, under the laundry hamper and even in his socks). He was quite creative in choosing hiding places but I would still find them and confront him with the evidence I found.

Matthew was a functional employee. He could get high and still hold on to his job. Unfortunately, the job didn't last too long because when you are in and out of jail, you can't be in two places at the same time. Eventually, he was fired and without that income we had to move into a studio apartment.

One evening, I was relaxing in a warm tub of water. I was at peace but always a little jittery because I never knew what was coming next. All of sudden the front door flew open. Matthew was screaming my name. From the sound of his voice I knew that he was in need of a fix. He charged into the bathroom and demanded $20.00! I quickly told him "I don't have that kind of money." He called me a liar and said, "I will kill you if you don't give it to me NOW!" He asked me "Where's your purse?" Before I could answer he had snatched me out of the tub and demanded that I give him some money!" I couldn't believe what I was going through and that this was happening to me. All of a sudden I felt a sharp object close to my naked skin. I was afraid to move or say the wrong thing because I knew if I did the sharp shiny blade would have cut deep into my throat.

Matthew dragged me to get my purse. I did manage to search for some money for him. Eight dollars was all that I found at the bottom of my purse. He snatched it out of my hand and in doing so he dropped the knife. He stormed out of the apartment and left the door wide opened. I stood there naked and crying. I vowed that evening *"that I was NOT going to suffer this pain ever again!"*

There would be many trials and tribulations I was to experience after that evening before freedom was to be mine. Not only was there a monkey on Matthew's back but the monkey was tearing the flesh off mine too. As a last ditch effort Matthew begged me to go with him to seek help. I soon realized that for some abusers, counseling just does not work. Addicts are habitual liars and manipulators. They could easily sell you sand at the beach. They're good! I totally believed Matthew was able to actually kick the habit.

I was only fooling myself again. We went to counseling and were told about a methadone program. The program was supposed to provide a safe and effective treatment to medically help him to withdraw and detox from the effects of his habit. I thought this treatment would cure his ingrained psychological dependence for heroin. The social worker also told me that in many situations like mine if a woman stays in the relationship she sometimes winds up using drugs too. She advised me not to stay with Matthew if he was not serious about helping himself.

Matthew was faithfully attending and participating in the methadone program by participating in its counseling sessions each week. The program requested weekly samples of urine from its participants for testing to determine if they were walking the straight and narrow (*were they clean drug free*).

As time progressed I found out that Matthew was still using. What was he doing with all the bottles of methadone that the clinic was giving him? He was selling them for ten dollars a bottle to buy more heroin. What a skillful game addicts play. I told you they are as slick as ice. No one can help a junkie, unless s/he wants help.

Matthew obviously didn't want it bad enough and my patience was running out. One morning I woke up and decided that I couldn't take this drama, stealing, lies, and his violent behaviors... anymore. My self-esteem and confidence were at an all-time low. I couldn't possibly love myself to allow a man to degrade and mistreat me like he was doing. I started making my plan to escape. Little by little, day-by-day, I began removing my personal possessions, mostly clothes and personal items from the apartment until most of them were gone. I was putting items in my purse before I left for work and putting them in my locker at school. All of this had to be done carefully and secretly so as not to draw attention to myself. I would space the few clothes that were left in the closet and spread them out so as not to look scarce. If he had any clue that I was planning to leave him, the violence would have escalated and there's no telling what he might have done. I really feared for my life and I had become a prisoner in my own space. After several months of strategic planning the day finally arrived. I looked around the four walls that had held such painful haunting memories for me and I closed the door behind me.

I was finally in a safe environment with Ken, a friend who was romantically interested in me but that's another whole story. I had nowhere else to go. I was scared to death Matthew would find me and kill me. He knew where all my familiar hangouts were located and where all my relatives and friends lived. I felt safe and protected staying with Ken and I was finally starting to feel like my old self again. I felt like all was going well for me and on the job too until one day I looked up and Matthew was suddenly standing over me. He looked as though he hadn't slept in days. He was unshaven. His clothes were wrinkled. He looked like a crazed mad person. I was embarrassed by the way he looked. He immediately let me know that he was furious that I walked out on him right under his nose. His behavior was erratic and he became verbally abusive. He was grabbing me and cursing at me. My co-workers were looking and wondering what was going on. Security personnel heard all the commotion and when they arrived, Matthew was escorted out of the building. He was still cursing and screaming. This embarrassing scene was played out for several days in the school's parking lot. It was more than I could handle. I decided it was time to take drastic measures AGAIN to ensure my safety and sanity. I knew I would have to come up with yet another plan.

I didn't realize how easy it was for a person to disappear. I was forced to take a thirty- day leave of absence from my job. No one knew where I was except for Ken, the friend I was staying with. I didn't tell my mother, family members or friends. I figured if they didn't know, they wouldn't have to lie or be intimidated by Matthew's insane behavior or threats. I was informed later "Matthew made several visits to everyone trying to find out where I was. It bothered me that I was worrying my family. I knew it hurt them not knowing where I was.

One day I had a doctor's appointment and when I came out of the office building my car was gone. As fate would have it, Matthew just happened to be in that area. He saw my car and he still had spare keys so he took the car. What are the chances of something like this happening? All the fears and insecurities that were slowly going away had reared their ugly heads again. I was a wreck. I was hysterical. I had no one to call but Ken. He tried to calm me down over the phone and said, "I'll leave work to come get you." I had no clue or idea where Matthew was with my car. He could be anywhere in a big city but I knew I had to find it. That was my car. I wanted it back!

Ken and I became a detective duo. We drove and combed various drug spots where Matthew was known to visit. It's funny how when you're on a mission and you're determined to accomplish something, all your fears go right out the window. For days we looked and searched for that car. Almost a week later we found it. The car was parked in front of a store. I immediately jumped out of Ken's car and ran to my car. I opened the door got in and drove away without any incidence or of Matthew seeing me. We wound up parking my car behind Ken's apartment building in the alley. I could not believe that I was living my life again as a prisoner in my own world, hiding my car and hiding myself.

An entire month went by when I decided to call Matthew's sister to see if it was safe to come out of hiding. She informed me that, "Matthew had left D.C. and was in California." I guess he finally decided that finding me was a lost cause. It was time to move on. My days as a victim were finally over. The year that I served in my personal war ended. Of course as in any war you still have to deal with its after effects. I still have a habit of looking at men's arms to see if there are any track (*needle*) marks from shooting heroin.

To this day I don't know what happened to Matthew. Whether or not he ever got his life straightened out, I'll never know. I spoke with a local attorney and he told me I could get a quick divorce by placing an add in a newspaper and if it was not disputed or challenged within 30 days then I was legally divorced. That sounds crazy doesn't it? Who knows I may still be married and since I have remarried I just might be committing a crime of polygamy. I haven't seen Matthew since he left and he never bothered to contact me again. I really don't know if he's dead or alive.

I did learn some valuable lessons that will stay with me forever. I became an enabler in a co-dependent relationship. (Ex: when Matthew's supervisor would call to see why he was late or not coming to work, I would make excuses for him. I would tell them that he was sick or that he had an emergency doctor's appointment.) In reality I lied for Matthew. I would give him money when he said he needed gas money. I knew damn well he was shooting it in his arms. I also made excuses for him to his family and my family when he would not show up for social gatherings. I knew he was somewhere getting high. This is not the way to help someone who is struggling with an addiction problem. I was a crutch for him. I was sending Matthew a message that it was okay for him to continue getting high and abusing me. Again, I was making excuses and protecting him so no one would suspect or know that he was doing drugs. Most importantly, I didn't want anyone to know how stupid I was to stay with him (*that's probably the real reason*). Remember, anyone can be an enabler whether it's drugs, gambling... or over-eating. It's all the same. As an enabler/co-dependent I prolonged his addiction. I was putting in the time to make the marriage work for him more than for myself. It was all about his comfort and convenience. My needs and wants were not in the equation at all. Existence in this unhealthy relationship could have caused me to be hospitalized or even killed. I was a fool for staying but it's easier said than done to leave. It is not an easy task to just pack up especially when you are not in control of the situation. Fear really plays a big factor.

If it were that simple, millions of women would just walk away and domestic violence would be a thing of the past. I don't know about your mother but mine made sure I understood that love meant giving of yourself without any limitations, not even when the circumstances say otherwise. She said, "In a relationship, you should stick by your partner. Never abandon them or bail out no matter what. Love is an unconditional commitment. You have to take the bitter with the sweet." I was taking all the bitter. This is why we must be very careful what seeds we plant in our daughter(s)' minds about love and relationships.

My Mom should have told me, "*Love and respect yourself first above everything else and that self-preservation is the first law of nature.*" Even though this might sound selfish, in actuality, I can only be responsible for me. You cannot protect or save others from their consequences that they have created out of their own actions. You cannot solve their problems for them, nor can you change anyone but yourself. In any relationship you should refuse to feel guilty and avoid surrendering your emotional balance for anyone.

"For better, for worse '*till death you do part*" should be banned from the wedding vows because the worse in some cases has over shadowed the better. "*Till death you do part*" seemed to be getting closer and closer everyday that I stayed married. The conversation between my mom and me should have been "*You are never to stay in a relationship that is not healthy*". I don't care what the marriage vows say! A lot of women go to their graves taking those vows to heart, but you've got to use some common sense too. You should not tolerate abuse under any circumstances just to say you have a man. If love means being treated less than human, you don't need it. Love is never ever supposed to hurt. You cannot fix other people. It is okay to walk away from a problematic relationship guilt free. Do I make myself perfectly clear? LOVE IS NEVER EVER UNDER ANY CIRCUMSTANCES SUPPOSED TO HURT OR MAKE YOU FEEL BAD!!!"

I guess if there were any important lessons learned, it would be to face and deal with your conflicts. If you don't acknowledge them, they will continue to escalate and will never be resolved. I spent all my time skirting around my issues doing anything to keep the peace at all cost. The price I paid was to live a nervous stressful unhappy lifestyle. That was too high a price to pay. I didn't have to put up and shut up but I chose to do that. Fear can and will make you do things you never thought you would do. In situations like mine it is best to contact and seek advice from an agency, organization or a professional clinician that specializes in domestic violence and substance abuse to get the support needed.

Remember, earlier I said, "That moving in with Ken was another whole story." Well, I figured you deserved to know how that turned out. We were in a relationship for a while and we also had a child together of which he denied being the father. After all we went through together, how could he? I still can't believe that he would abandon me like that. Some men will tell you that they love you, can't live with out you and as soon as the heat and pressure is on, they run like the cowards they are. He talked a good game but he didn't back it up.

After the baby was born I hired an attorney to serve him papers to prove paternity. It's funny because after that, he mysteriously admitted that it was his child. He needed to pay child support and I wasn't going to let him off the hook easily. Eighteen years later he only saw his daughter once and since then I have not heard from him. He paid the price but I was still left to raise our child by myself. Lesson learned? Use birth control!

**Tell your daughters to be careful with who they lie down with!**

Before your daughter starts dating, talk to her about healthy relationships and what to look for in a romantic partner. One in ten teens have been physically abused by a boyfriend or girlfriend. Prevention should be the rule of thumb rather than intervention.

It's better to teach them about dating and relationships early on in hopes that they will be able to identify the signs that a partner may have violent tendencies. Inform them that many teens and adult women are in relationships that are or can become physically abusive.

## What To Bring To The Table

- ➢ Discuss with them how one should be treated in a relationship.
- ➢ Ask them "How do you feel when you are with that person?"
- ➢ When a relationship doesn't feel good, be able to identify it (ex: possessiveness, jealousy, excessive calling or texting, sharing embarrassing information on social networks, verbal/mental/emotional or physical abuse, not allowed to have friends or other interests outside of the relationship, ... to name a few)
- ➢ Do not choose a mate based on their physical attributes. That's shallow. It's nice that s/he looks good and has a nice body but what else does s/he have to offer to the relationship? (ex: intelligence, humor, sensitivity, respect, morals and values)
- ➢ Be a role model by treating your daughter(s) and others with respect. Think about your own behaviors. Determine if your values match the same values you are trying to teach.

If you suspect your child, or if you are a victim of domestic/relationship violence get help. Make contact with your local domestic/violence prevention organization.

## Be a Victor not a Victim

# eight

# What You Do in the Dark Will Come out in the Light

"The truth will always find you when you least expect it, whether you're ready or not. I came face to face with it. It wasn't a pretty picture. It's funny how one piece of paper could change your whole life. *"What you do in the dark will come out in the light"* The secret my husband tried to hide in the dark was now in the light. It was shining like a spotlight in my face.'

*Cheryl Patterson, 60 years old, Springfield, Illinois*

You often hear people talk about the *"Good Ole Days."* Those were the days when kids were kids. We had pajama parties (*girls only of course*), skating parties and house parties (*called quarter parties you pay a quarter to get in*). After school we would hang out at the recreational center and socialize. It was just good clean fun. Life was fairly simple then. We all looked out for each other like brothers and sisters. We were protective of each other. Violence and disrespect among us was unheard of. If there was a problem, we talked it out and settled it. If there was a fight it was one on one and then it was squashed and no retaliations were involved. In fact most times you became friends with the person you were at odds with.

There is one thing that has not changed much between then and now. It's in the dating/relationship department. The guys are still the same *(smooth talkers that want to get in your pants, like bees to honey)*. You know the kind that will say, *"I love you."* or *"If you really loved me you would give me some."* I dated quite a bit and I started in my freshman year. Believe me, most of them tried to get the prize *(my virginity)* but I wasn't having it. They weren't going to have bragging rights and build a reputation on me.

Well, that was short lived but at least I held out until my senior year of high school. I fell prey to one of those smooth talking operators. He was cute, popular and persistent. He said, "I really like you. You're so pretty. I only want to be with you and nobody else." He was filling my head with all his lies and flattery. Of course I believed him. All those years of holding out and I fell hard to his lines of lies.

I had heard other girls talk about protection to keep from getting pregnant. When I asked him about wearing a condom, his response was "I can't wear one because I won't be able to feel anything." Something tells me that this is the same line that is being used today. Ha, a millennium later and some things still never change. He said, "I want you. You are special to me." I was so smitten by him that I eventually gave in and had unprotected sex. I only had sex with Keith once and that was enough for him. Keith got what he wanted and then he dropped me like a hot potato.

I graduated in June of that year and was looking forward to getting a job and taking some college courses. I was really excited about that but those plans were soon put aside. As the old story goes my mind couldn't believe I was pregnant but my body told me I was. I didn't need a test or a doctor to figure that out. I tried to hide it from my mother but I had morning sickness real bad. I was throwing up everything. I should have known that a mother's tuition/radar is always on and better than any psychic or doctor. It was too late she already knew.

During the time I was growing up, if you were pregnant and single that was unacceptable. It was a social taboo. Your family and those in the community shamed you. It was nothing to be excited about or proud of. You were considered an easy girl, a whore, and a tramp. Unlike growing up today, it seems more acceptable to give birth as a teen. It is well celebrated with baby showers and parties whether the young lady knows the father or not. There is nothing to be ashamed of anymore.

Once it was established that I was pregnant, my mother and I went back and forth about taking Keith to court to provide child support. I really didn't want to be bothered or even see him again. I just wanted to be left alone. Money did become an issue because my mother didn't make a lot of money and I wasn't working. We, eventually decided that it wasn't an option and off to court we went. It was the most hurtful and embarrassing experience I ever had. In the court room in front of everybody Keith denied that he was the father of my child. He stated that I had been with other boys beside him. How could he? He knew that I was a virgin. He was the only person I ever had sex with. I knew then for sure that he wanted nothing to do with me or the child he had fathered. I guess I wasn't special to him anymore. I guess he didn't love me after all. I had fallen for the oldest trick in the world; believing the ole "*I love you*" game.

Right then and there I knew how dramatically my life was about to change.

My dreams of living happily ever after like the children's story, Cinderella," and being swept off my feet by my prince charming was only a fairy tale. I now had real life responsibilities. I was a single parent. The fun and games of my young life were over. It was time to be a mother and raise my child. There was not going to be someone to come along and save me.

There were some options presented to me that I should have taken advantage of at that time that might have assisted me with my child. I had an offer to move to Iowa with an aunt and attend nursing school. I chose not to go to because I had visited there before and for some reason I didn't feel comfortable around my aunt's husband. I felt like he was always looking at me up and down as if he wanted to sop me up like a biscuit with syrup. Years later, I found out that he had sexually assaulted one of my younger cousins on a regular basis who had lived there with her mother for a short time. I then had another offer to live in California and stay with my godparents. That was a long way from home and I didn't want to be that far away from my mom. It seems that I closed the window of opportunity on both chances. Always remember should've, would've and could've will never make anything happen in your life. You have to step up take charge and make a decision that will better your situation. Some of you may think this is selfish but sometimes we need to put ourselves first. In order to reach your full potential it is imperative that your needs be addressed. You must determine what it is you want and deserve out of life and then go after it.

### Living Guilt Free Produces a Healthy State of Mind!

➢ Let go. Free yourself from others who judge you and make unrealistic demands of you and your time.
➢ Have respect for your own feelings, desires and needs.
➢ Nurture and love yourself.
➢ Celebrate your accomplishments no matter how big or small. If you don't love yourself, who will?

### Who's In Charge? Who Runs The Show?

➢ If you want a better life, you have to want it and want it badly.

➤ Tune out those inner voices that tell you that success is impossible. If you listen to them long enough, you will start to believe them.

➤ Changing your mindset doesn't happen overnight. It takes time to reverse all those years of erroneous thinking.

➤ Each day commit to a life-changing plan of action that will put you in control of fulfilling your goals/intentions.

### The Sacrificial Lamb: The High Price You Pay When You Devalue Yourself

➤ When we fail to take care of #1 (put your needs first), we tend to forfeit/exhaust the time and energy necessary to pursue and follow our own agenda.

➤ When you become a sacrificial lamb, you are ignoring your desires/needs in order to fulfill the desires/needs of others.

➤ People will drain you if you allow them to. They will take and take and give nothing in return. They will make decisions for you and tell you what's best for you.

➤ "Strike while the Iron is hot." When a positive opportunity presents itself to you weigh your choices then take full advantage before you lose that chance.

I was afraid to step away from my family. I needed the safety net of my mother and siblings to survive. I often wondered what it would have been like to leave my anchored roots and start all over. Please, I don't want you to think I'm having a well-attended pity party. I'm not. I just want to make a point. In some instances we can eliminate some of the stressors/pressures that we bring into our lives. This can be achieved by not becoming a caretaker to everybody. Be a little selfish. Pamper yourself from time to time. If you give everything away all the time, you will have nothing left for yourself.

My mother and aunts kept telling me "Hurry up and find a good man to marry to take care of you and the baby." They stated "It's not going to be easy because what man wants a ready-made family?" Back then that was true. You were considered used goods. It was only a couple of months later when a guy I knew from high school came home for a furlough from his tour of duty from the military. I had always thought of him as real cool and good looking and he looked especially good in his uniform. He was a gentleman and he was always respectful. I knew that he had always dated older women. I was sure he would never take a second look at me since I was fifteen years younger than he was. Well, he did take that second look at me. We started dating and I was on cloud nine. It seemed like I was finally going to have some happiness in my life.

Tony was only home for a short time before he had to leave for his final tour of duty. It did allow us to spend some time together getting to know each other better. What we found out was that we didn't have a lot of things in common. In fact we didn't have anything in common. He was much older than I, he was well traveled and I was still at home. I was the small town girl who had never seen a big city or been too many places. I liked to go out and he liked to stay home. I guess none of that matters when someone is good to you and treats you like a lady. At least that's what I thought, but you really need more than that to make a solid relationship.

Tony knew the hardships I was going through. I was in court fighting for child support and trying to take care of a baby by myself. When he returned home, he told me that I didn't have to go through that anymore. He said, "I will take care of the baby and you." He asked me to marry him. I felt really blessed and at the same time relieved that my knight in shining armor was going to rescue me. Or was he?

My mother and aunts were ecstatic that I had found a man that was going to marry a young girl with a baby. No men back then wanted a ready-made family especially a baby born from another man. They kept telling me, "Girl you better hurry and marry him before he changes his mind. You're not going to find anything better" I heard that statement so much I actually started believing it. Just a word of advice, NEVER marry a man because you or everybody else thinks he's a good catch. I'll tell you why. I didn't realize it at the time, but I didn't have to get married. I could have very well taken care of the baby by myself. I didn't need a man to do that for me. Mama always told my sisters and me "Whatever you wanted in your lives had to take a back seat when it comes to your husband and children because they were the most important." RED FLAG! RED FLAG! Whatever you do, please don't tell you daughter(s) this. It is detrimental and damaging to the psyche. You might as well tell her "*She's invisible.*" A woman should never under any circumstances live in the shadows of a man. Our goals, ambitions, interests, and feelings are just as important as his. Nor, should we take on the role of the dutiful doting wife.

I watched my mom closely growing up in her house and she ran it like a business. She was a perfectionist. I mean everything had to be in order. There was no room for error. I was led to believe that if I didn't do things correctly or up to her standards, I was a failure. Who wants to be labeled a failure? The pressure and stakes that she held were too high and impossible to meet. Unfortunately, my feelings of fear and insecurities of being perfect followed me right into adulthood.

Sometimes I would have great ideas that I thought were exciting. When I shared my dreams or ideas, I would always get negative feedback and comments from my mother and especially my husband. They would tell me "You can't do that. You don't have the money to get it done, you don't have the intelligence, and this will be impossible for you to achieve." I would hear this more often than I care to repeat. I just gave up on my dreams/ideas before even getting started. Every time I came with an idea that was marketable I was talked out of it. A lot of things that I initially saw in my mind have now been patented. Not by me but by others who had the perseverance and guts to carry out their ideas. I should have learned if you do fail, so what, it's okay. It's not the end of the world. Whatever idea or dream is given to you is meant just for you and not for them. I'm pressing the pause button for a minute to make this point.

### Catch A Dream And Hold On To It

Kids do not understand that there are no limitations on dreaming. Their minds have not been poisoned and tainted with thoughts of doubts and fears. They believe that anything is possible. As mothers we should not deny our children's right to dream. If we do deny them the right to dream, their chances to achieve will be short lived.

Everyone has a special talent and is good at something. It is up to us to help them find that gift. NEVER tell them their dreams are stupid or not important. We want to develop our daughter(s)' self-confidence, not tear it down. Allow them to think they can do or be anything they want. Look around you today and see the roles and positions that women have taken on. Some things we would have never thought that a woman could ever have achieved, have been done. Allow them to believe in themselves. We know that there will be enough people who will knock them down and tell them they can't fulfill their dreams. They don't need us for that. Your job is to be a dream catcher and cheer them on.

### IF YOU LEAD THEY WILL FOLLOW

What examples are you setting for your children? Our children are always looking to us for assistance, directions, and guidance. They emulate whatever they see us doing. Their eyes are always watching. If you crush their spirits before they can even begin on their road to success, it will negatively carry over into her adult life and impact the things she wants to accomplish.

### READY SET GO... ACTION

It's never too early to develop a plan of action. Start asking your daughter(s) how they plan to reach their goals. What are the steps needed to get things moving? Let them know that nothing is written in stone and life has no guarantees. You don't just wake up and something happens. We have to put in place those strategies to make things happen. Your daughter(s) will show interests in many different things including careers. As they mature and develop, they will eventually narrow those interests down to a few and give more attention to specific ones.

Take an active role in exposing them to various activities and life experiences to broaden their horizons. Everybody can't win an Oscar. You will win some. You will lose some. This is just part of life. We all fall down but the beauty of it is we can get back up. When we make mistakes, they become learning experiences that we can use as a frame of reference in making future choices and decisions. Building a foundation to success means learning from our mistakes.

It does hurt us when we see our children cry, become hurt/injured or they are met with defeats. We probably hurt more than they do. It's interesting that while we are still internalizing their pain, they have moved on to something or someone else. They are resilient and will rebound. None of us can avoid the disappointments of life. We need to allow our daughters to experience the good times and the bad because that's what life is about. Help them to realize that some dreams may not arrive or come easily. Teach them not to give up when life sometimes kicks us in our lower posterior. Teach them to keep their boxing gloves on. You have twelve rounds to fight for what you want. No matter what the outcome might be, keep fighting.

Guess I took my boxing gloves off because I gave up the fight and became lost in my family. I started living though my children's lives, especially my husband's. In my marriage it seemed like I was the one that was always submissive. Whatever he wanted, he got it. If we went to the movies, it was always what Tony wanted to see. If we went out to eat it was always where and what he wanted to eat. I realized that I was always putting my needs and interests aside for his sake. Why do we as women put up with this shit! I guess when you marry young you can be molded into this person that your mate wants you to be. I needed someone to tell me that I was important too but this wasn't happening.

It took me a while to figure this out but you don't need anyone to tell you that you're important. That's something you have to do for yourself but it is nice to hear it from your man sometime like "Honey, what is it you want? What do you need? What can I do to make you happy?" I became the dutiful wife trying to be everything to everybody. Tony was enjoying his life and I was living my life for him.

One day I was doing laundry and I happened to see one of Tony's shirts fall on the floor. I bent down to pick it up and I noticed there was something in the pocket. Now, before you jump to conclusions, I was not snooping or looking for anything but it was looking for me. I got real excited because I thought it was some money. Instead, when I reached into the pocket I found a letter that was folded up. I didn't think anything of it. I opened it and read it. My eyes couldn't believe what I was reading. It was a summons for him to appear in court for child support. I became totally numb. I was devastated. My world, in a matter of seconds was completely shattered. The man who I had been faithful to for years was not only having an affair but he had also fathered a child too! I immediately began to rationalize and think maybe I was reading this wrong or maybe it was another Tony not my Tony. I started justifying to myself that I had been the perfect wife and mother and that he would never play around on me. There was no mistake here. What he did in the dark had finally come out into the light. The secret my husband tried to hide was now in the light and it was shining brightly in my face.

He was good, damn good about hiding this affair and child from the kids and me for all these years. How did he do it? I had no clue of what was happening. I'll tell you how good he was. He kept it a secret for fifteen years. That's how old his son was when I found the summons. That means he had covered his steps masterfully! Can you imagine having another woman and a baby without anyone knowing? Not even his family! Well, it can and does happen. I'm a living witness. You can be slick all you want but somewhere somehow you're going to slip up and he finally did. I tried to make sense of this but it was too much for my mind to handle. Luckily for him he wasn't home at the time because you know what the ending would have been.

I was cool. When he got home, I immediately confronted him with the letter. He had the nerve to deny the contents and told me "That letter wasn't for me and I don't have a child!" How stupid did he think I was? He continued this foolish dialogue even though the truth was staring him in the face. Of course things dramatically changed after that because the trust factor was gone. I wondered how many other women he had been with and what other women felt in situations like this. How did they manage a cheating husband? Did they seek counseling? Did they leave or stay with him? I know many women have gone through this crisis. Infidelity didn't just start yesterday. It's been around for a long time but you never think it will happen to you. I do have just one question that maybe you can answer. Why is it acceptable for men to cheat yet frowned upon if women do the very same thing? From what I remember the answer is "A woman can't do what a man can and still be a lady. If a man screws around that's a badge of honor but if a woman does it she's a hoe."

My self-confidence went straight to hell. I began thinking about what this woman was like to lure my husband into bed with her. What did she have that I didn't. I wanted to know if she was sexy, was she attractive, was she better looking than me? Did she have more education? Was she supplying his emotional needs? I really wanted to know what led him into the arms of another woman. I tortured myself and suffered through the emotional trauma of betrayal, deception, humiliation, and mixed feelings of anger and sadness. He's been caught with his pants down so where do my children and I go from here? Hold it for a minute. There is more drama to come!

When reality sets in, your emotions subside. The initial shock wears off (*You think it never will, but eventually it does.*) It's time to deal with the truth and determine how you will survive the infidelity.

### Stay Or Go? That Is The Question

➢ You need some space and some "me" time right now to sort out and harness your raging emotions.
➢ It's not a good idea to make any concrete decisions right away because you're probably not thinking clearly. The last thing you want to do is to make hasty choices that you might regret later.

### Choose An Unbiased Support Group

➢ Your girlfriends and relatives are going to be the first to give you advice and tell you what to do. Ask them "What University they received their marriage/family counseling degree and license from?"
➢ Seek a certified therapist or life coach. They will be neutral and have experience in listening. They will be able to assist you in making clear rational decisions.

### Stick With Your Program

➢ "Don't fake it until you make it." Whatever activities you were doing before, keep doing them.
➢ Take care of yourself even if you do not feel like it.
➢ Continue maintaining good clean healthy nutrition, drink water and exercise this is crucial for your well-being. Get those facials, nails and hair done. You want to look good in case you decide to leave his raggedy ass or meet someone else.

### Rome Wasn't Built In A Day

> ➤ There is a process toward healing. It takes time to rebuild trust and to recommit to the relationship (*if that's what you want to do*).
> ➤ It's not easy but love yourself through this process. Don't punish or beat yourself up for someone else's mistake.
> ➤ There's no "quick fix" to repair any relationship that has been damaged. It is up to you to conclude what the final outcome will be.
> ➤ As with any challenges you face, this too shall pass. You deserve the time and space necessary to heal. You will smile again!

I continued to confront Tony with questions about his affair. When I found out the woman he had an affair with was his co-worker, I was livid. I started thinking and thinking about what I was going to do. I really wanted to leave him but where would I go? I had no skills, no money, two children in college, and one in middle school. I had spent my whole life as a caretaker and never prepared myself for a career or profession. I had depended on Tony all my life. How would I make it on my own? I was making up reasons and excuses why I shouldn't leave. I realized that I was doing it again putting everyone else in front of me. It was difficult not to when my mother and aunts had drilled it in my head "Be a good wife. Stay at home and Let your husband take care of you." They had crippled me. I believed I could not make it without a man. I bought into that shit!

I look at pictures of my grandmother. She looked so tired and unhappy. I never saw a picture of her smiling, just looking worn out. Just like me she married at a very young age of 16 and had nine children. I know that at that age she didn't have a clue about being a mother and a wife. I remember my aunt telling me that my grandmother married so that she could be taken care of and provided for. It's been said that in some cases history repeats itself until somebody consciously changes it. It is not the norm for a man to take care of you but it was in my mother's case. I guess that's why my mother never remained single after her two divorces. Her mental state was brainwashed into believing, "Find a man who will take charge and care for you (*lesson learned, unfortunately for me a little bit too late*)."

Each day I became more and more depressed. I would cry for hours. I started feeling sorry for myself. I wanted to find some-body... anybody to talk about what I was going through. I wanted someone like Tony had...someone to hold me, kiss me, and make me feel good...but I was not that type of woman. I had always been a one-man woman. I was the perfect wife, mother, and was always faithful. Where did that get me? Sometimes, as women, we settle and accept bits and pieces of a man and a relationship. We get along just to get along. We figure having a broke down man is better than not having a man at all. It is pitiful what we will put up with. I know a lot of women out there are *"putting up."*

When you have sex with a married man, get pregnant, give birth YOU officially become a *"baby mama"* but get something straight, it doesn't mean the father belongs to you now or ever. Let me tell you what this *"heifer"* did. This is where the drama and blatant disrespect began. Once Nita discovered that I knew about the affair and the baby, she started harassing and stalking me I'm really surprised that she didn't try and contact me before now. Most women would have wanted to mess things up on the home front.

On my way to work I happened to look through my rear view mirror. I noticed that every time I changed lanes, a blue car that was behind me would change lanes too. I didn't want to be para-noid but when you are driving and make a turn and the car behind you follows, you start wondering what is going on. I pulled into my parking lot at work but the car following me kept going. I slowed down to see who the driver was but they sped away and I couldn't see. This went on for several days. Finally, I could see the driver was definitely a woman. Something wasn't right. I decided to tell Tony about this incident. I had my suspicions that it was Nita. After sharing my *"paranoia"* with Tony, he told me the type of car that Nita drove. I knew then it was her. I told him, "that I was not going to be playing any games with her. You need to check her and straighten this shit out NOW!"

The next couple of days I noticed that she was still following me, as if I didn't know she was there. Of course you know this was not the end of it. She started calling the house and hanging up when I answered. How juvenile can you be (*A grown woman playing these stupid ass games*)? Again, I went to Tony and informed him of what Nita was doing. She continued to call and said, "Tony and I are still sleeping together. He really wants to be with me but you won't divorce him. That's why he's still there with you." She promised me, "In the end I will have him all to myself." I couldn't believe this fool was ranting on and on. I was beyond angry. I was in the fighting mad mode and wanted to kick some ass. You always hear about these kind of crazy women who think they can take your man from you but she was going to be sadly mistaken. I had given him the best years of my life and there was no way in hell she was going to take that away from me!

About a week later I was leaving work on a Friday and when I got to my car it was sitting on four flat tires and the windows were shattered. She had the nerve to leave some pictures in an envelope of Tony, her and the baby in the front seat of the car. I called a cab because I couldn't get Tony on the phone. When I got home he was there. I was beyond angry and I made it very clear that if he didn't handle Nita I would. Then I decided I wasn't going to wait on him because obviously whatever he was saying to this idiot bitch was not working. All of these incidents that were happening were starting to scare me. I guess this was her intention. You hear about stories of women who stalk their lovers and their wives all the time and some of them turn into disasters.

Out of fear I went on-line, found the nearest gun shop and purchased a 25 caliber. This was just enough to protect myself. I would use it if I had to. I could see what Nita was capable of doing. I remember the saying *"Hell hath no fury like a woman scorned."* Owning a gun is one thing, but using it is another. With that comes responsibility and if there is one thing that I have learned in life it is about making choices. I didn't want to do something out of fear so I decided to first get a restraining order against Nita. Although, that doesn't always stop someone from stalking you, at least it is a start. Things did get better with the order of protection and knowing that I had the gun. Well fortunately I didn't have to use it. Nita finally came to her senses and all the craziness slowly stopped. I guess Tony let her know that he was not going to leave his wife and children and that I had a gun and didn't have a problem using it!!! I still wonder why some women think just because they have slept with a married man or had his child that he is going to leave his wife and be with her *(pathetic)*.

With all I had gone through, I did find a way to deal with my pain but not a good one. I was always a good cook and the kitchen became my friend. I started baking cookies, cakes, and pies. I was eating them as fast as I was making them. I became an emotional eater and the food became my friend and consoler. I couldn't stop because it was masking the pain and deadening it. I gained forty pounds. All those cookies and cakes I was eating didn't come close to ending my inner burden. In fact, it added to it. When I looked in the mirror or saw pictures of myself, I like my grandmother could see the unhappiness and sadness that I alone had created.

In order to regain and stabilize my sanity, I had to forgive Tony. If you refuse to forgive, it will consume you and you will never have any peace of mind. I've been told that you're supposed to do both, forgive and forget but I will never forget. Tony made a point of begging me not to leave him. He tried to sell me the ideas that it was just a moment of weakness *(bull shit)*. I stayed anyway. After all, at this point in my life where would I go? I had put twenty-five years of sweat and tears into this relationship, even though he had destroyed our marriage. He was the only man I knew so I decided to stay. Even though I never really loved him I didn't want to be alone (*remember I got married for convenience*).

Let your daughters know that being alone is not a death sentence. It's okay to spend time getting to know who you are. This is an opportunity to further explore personal interests and work on "*self*". You should never look for a man to complete you. You should always complete each other.

It has been a long and difficult road. Often times, I still find myself saying, "I should have left Tony." Staying in a marriage just because... is not reason enough to stay. Both parties lose and no one is happy. I can't change the past. You can only live in the present and live one day at a time. The future will take care of itself. Nothing is promised but I know that God is not finished with me yet. I have a lot of living to do. Age will not stop anyone from accomplishing whatever it is s/he wants to do. Each experience in life happens for a reason. There are many lessons to be learned on this earth plane. These experiences help us to grow, mature, and become a better person. Life is like school. You are promoted to the next grade level as you learn each life's lessons. Each challenge that you overcome moves you on to the next grade. The bottom line is to do what makes you happy and live life to the fullest. I realize that now but it took me a lifetime to learn. I know I'm not a selfish person and I have learned that I don't have to put everyone else ahead of me anymore.

I think back sometimes to what my mother said about my grandmother, "All she did was cook and do chores." She had no enjoyment or opportunity to step outside of her role. She never took the time to give her children a hug or tell them she loved them. Her time was spent keeping all the balls in the air by keeping the household going and taking care of her husband and children. How sad! That's why I made sure my children got plenty of love. Most importantly, I tried to share with them lessons that I missed growing up. Whether they took heed or not at least I can say, *"I gave the lessons to them."* I talk to my young granddaughters frequently because I know there's a lot of peer pressure out there. Each generation has its share. I hope they feel they can come to me with any questions or concerns that they may have. Always be as open as possible with your daughters. We have lived through most of the things in life they are now experiencing so they can benefit from our mistakes. Don't allow them to roam around feeling their way in the dark. That's why you're there, to turn on the lights.

Again, make it plain to them, *"You are capable of accomplishing anything you want."* Stress to them *"You can do this on your own. You don't need a man to take care of you."* We also have to inform our young men too how important it is that if they become a father to a child or children, you are obligated and responsible to take care of that child as well as be in their lives. Men please step up and be counted!

As for me, I am going to live my life daily like it's my last. "Set backs" don't mean *"get back."* It means to *"re-set"* and move forward. I have talked to many women and read their stories about husbands who were unfaithful and how they have managed to overcome that part of their life. That's why I wanted to tell my story in hopes that something I said would touch someone and be of encouragement to them. It only takes a few words to motivate one into action.

When you listen to your inner voice, it will help guide you to your purpose. Until then we are always where we are supposed to be at any given time. I have a new attitude and I am on a mission to be the person God wants me to be. I think of myself as a cocoon that will continue to blossom into a beautiful butterfly. I wake up every day excited that it's my turn now. I'm going to love me, do me, and please me. I know that I will never put myself in second place again.

Of course if I had known what I know now I would have taken that chance and moved to California with my baby and hopefully done a lot of things differently. At least I could have taught her about being independent and taking risks. Hindsight is always 20/20. You should always try, and if you fail, try again or better yet try something else.

I have one particular inspirational reading that is a favorite of mine that I will share with you. "Consider your past through the eyes of the Spirit. See every choice in a light of love. Give thanks for every experience. Forgive every mistake and every wrong doing because your good resides only in the present moment not in the past". How enlightening and healing these words are. Each of you, are delicate jewels and should be treated as such. *Don't cut or short-change yourself.*

I often use affirmations to confirm and remind me of who I am. "I am a strong, intelligent, beautiful woman. I release the past and move forward knowing that I am blessed." Love and blessings to each of you and...

**May you find your special place in life. You deserve it.**

*nine*

# 357 Magnum Date from Hell

"I was just a small town country girl who grew
up in a strict sheltered *"Mama"* proof house. I was
naive about men, relationships, and especially
SEX. I was always book smart but short on street
smarts. Sometimes, you have to learn street smarts
on your own. Realistically, you need a balance
between the two. Thanks to the feminist movement, my old fashioned thinking about men and
sex were soon abandoned. I was introduced to free
love and the door to my sexual prison was opened.
Even though I was still not *"ready for the world,"* I
wanted to be an independent woman. With that new
found freedom came some experiences and consequences that I was in no way prepared or ready
for including a .357 revolver held to my head."

*Ann Marie Jackson, 46 years old, Jacksonville, Florida*

Mama was raised before the feminist movement began. There was
never much talk about women's rights. There were never any discussions on the subjects of self-acceptance, independence or self-
esteem. It was out of the question for a woman to think she could

129

be assertive or have control over her life. Most women just didn't do that. They were taught early on to stay in their place, which meant raise the children and commit to memory, the wedding vows to *"honor and obey"*. Thank goodness that has been removed from the wedding ceremony.

When I was twelve years old I remember Mama hitting my Dad over the head with a skillet (*not one of those lightweight Teflon coated pan*), but one of those heavy cast-iron skillets that was used to make homemade cornbread in. Once again, she had uncovered his cheating habits. I remember hearing Mama on the telephone telling her best friend of her husband's latest indiscretions, not knowing that her best friend was loving daddy too. I heard all kinds of stories of his womanizing and that daddy had even dated his own cousin.

Daddy was a handsome man, a real looker and definitely a ladies' man. How did I know that at twelve years old? It was simple. First of all most little girls love and adore their daddies. Second of all everywhere we went women would always speak to him, smile at him, wink at him, and sometimes they would scribble something on small pieces of paper or on the inside of a matchbook cover and give it to him. I didn't know what was on the small pieces of paper or on the inside of the matchbook covers, but whatever it was, it made Daddy smile. As I got older I realized they were giving him their names and telephone numbers. He would say to me, "Don't tell your Mama what you saw." I struggled to understand why I wasn't supposed to tell but as I look back it was because he didn't want to be in more trouble with mama and get another knock up side his head.

From what he put her through I now realize that a woman can only take so much mental and emotional abuse before her self-esteem or self-worth is affected. The lack of self-esteem or self-worth can be damaging and shake the very core of your existence. Self-esteem determines how you feel about yourself. It begins first in the home environment. You can't inherit it and you can't buy it. When your self-esteem is low, it can lead to depression and an inability to reach your full potential. In some cases it will allow you to become tolerant to abusive situations and relationships. I guess the latter affected Mama.

Daddy continued his endless habit of engaging in intimate relationships outside of his marriage to my mom. As time progressed my mom realized that there wasn't much she could do about it. She finally gave up and let go. Her self-esteem began to deteriorate little by little. Unfortunately, it took a toll on me too. Her problem became my problem and it grew into some things later on that I was unable to handle. I'll tell you about that shortly.

There's one thing about the lack of self-esteem, you never seem to be satisfied with who you are. You start believing and thinking, "I'm too fat," "I'm too skinny," "I'm too tall," "I'm too short," "I wish I had long hair," I wish I had curly hair," just to name a few. All these things can affect you when you don't feel good about your physical appearance or have a poor body image. It becomes difficult in valuing who you really are. It's only a natural desire to feel accepted but sometimes we care more about how others see us than how we see ourselves. Feeling good about your self has a direct affect on how you act, think, and socialize...

### How Does Your Body Image Measure Up?

Are you always comparing yourself to others? Some people compare themselves to actors, entertainers or celebrities they see on TV, movies and magazines. It's not easy trying to be like someone else. You cannot measure yourself against others because there is only one y-o-u and that spells YOU.

### Growing Pains Are A Pain In The - - -

Growing pains occur when mothers' are critical of how their daughters' look. Mothers, relatives, peers, and friends may make negative comments, or make condescending remarks about their bodies. This can be hurtful as well as harmful to the child's self-esteem. This can cause them to become more self-conscious when they reach puberty. We want to spend more time encouraging self-acceptance by praising and providing positive feedback to uplift them.

> Let your daughter(s) know that puberty is part of growing up and becoming a woman. It is an important stage in her life when the body is developing. It is not an easy or simple process. Take the time to explain so she will know what to expect.

> Inform her that, "Our society is obsessed with physical appearances which may cause many young girls to feel uncomfortable in their own bodies." The obsessions may result in serious negative actions/behaviors such as developing eating disorders or holding onto to unrealistic images.

> The media continues to portray the ideal female as thin and sexy. Young girls may feel they have to live up to this image. There are some things about yourself that you can't change. Even the celebrities that you think are perfect find imperfections about themselves. Looks are deceiving.

> You are BODYLICIOUS. When you speak negative comments about yourself, you are declaring to the universe that you are not important. When you start to put yourself down, say, "STOP!" and give yourself a compliment. I know you can find something good about yourself or something that you do well. Remember, there is no one on this earth like you. You are a special VIP.

> Always focus on the positive things going on in your life. Concentrate on the things that make you happy. This will help you to change how you think and feel about yourself.

Speaking of feeling good about your self, it took mama seventeen years to finally leave my Dad. I wondered did it ever dawn on her that she didn't have to subject herself to the disrespect and the necessary ride on that emotional roller coaster. I didn't know that some men would not and could not handle monogamous relationships, married or not. I learned from my observations that you are not always the only honey in the jar. Some men always keep a spare one around.

I was a chunky child growing up. Mama always covered it up by telling me, *"you're not fat, just big boned."* Food was always plentiful and I began to eat until I could almost feel my fat cells burst. I think I ate to cover up the pain of watching my parents arguing, seeing their marriage fall apart, and just plain boredom. I was an only child so I didn't have any siblings to do things with and friends were scarce because no one wanted to hang out with a fat girl so I found comfort in food. It was my friend. It didn't judge me.

At a time in life when a teen is discovering and searching for their identity, mine was nowhere to be found. I never felt I was smart enough, pretty enough, small enough or good enough for anyone or anything. As I continued to eat I was no longer just *big boned I was fat.* Then mama and daddy started telling me that, "You'd better stop eating so much or you'll never have a boyfriend". Boy, did that hurt because, I wanted so bad to look cute like the rest of the other girls at school. I was always comparing myself to other girls my age. I wanted to be them (*That's where self-esteem steps in.*). The only thing I understood from the life I was living was that North America's standards were not accepting of fat dark-skinned girls. I thought to myself, you're right mama why would any man want me? By the time I was fourteen years old, my body image had been totally destroyed. I was literally big as a house. Starting high school was a disaster for me; especially where the boys were concerned. They wanted the little petite cutie girls with the long hair and so I was left out. Dating was not an option for me.

It's always been said that high school are the best years of your life. I decided I wasn't going to let my fat butt miss out on all that fun, especially the parties, dating, and sex (*that was still questionable*).

I told my mother that I wanted to lose weight and would she take me to the doctor to get some help. The doctor prescribed some amphetamines (*diet pills*) and water pills. I was popping pills every-day and that fat melted off my body like ice cream. In less than four months I was looking like a movie star. I had a little part time job so I had money of my own. This allowed me to buy all new sexy clothes. I broke loose, I was lookin good and nobody could tell me nothin. It seemed as though the floodgates opened and the boys at my school were coming at me from everywhere, they were all over me but I put the brakes on and wouldn't talk to any of them. I told them, "You didn't want me when I was fat, so you don't want me now." It felt so good to tell them that. No matter how hard they con-tinued to try to get with me my answer was still no. I started dating guys from other high schools that I would meet at parties, skating, football/basketball games, and other social events. I was running in the fast lane drinkin, smoking, (*everything but the sex, that would come much later*).

Speaking on the topic of sex I think back to what mama said. She would always chant her favorite mantra to me over and over and over and I'm sure most women in my age group have heard it. "*Keep your dress down and your panties up.*" Now, you tell me what sense this would make to a ten-year-old child (*that's when I first heard it*). She bombarded me with books to explain "*the facts of life*" But if you don't know what you're reading you still have no idea of what's going on. From what I've been told discussions about sex by some mothers are still off limits today. Some mothers don't even give out the books anymore.

I recall asking my aunts what Mama meant when she said, "Keep your dress down and your panties up." I hit a brick wall there too. They would say, "You don't need to know nothing about that girl." The women in my family would always preach to me that boys were only interested in fast girls for only one reason and that was for sex. It seemed no one wanted to educate me on this sex thing. In my young circle of friends we depended upon each other for the facts of life. We wrote our own rules of what we thought was the truth and we lived by them. Our mothers had already told us some of the myths or lies. For example, *"You could get pregnant by kissing a boy"*. *"If you slow danced with a boy, you will get pregnant"*. *"If you let a boy lay on top of you, you'll get pregnant."* and of course the all-time favorite was *"Babies were delivered by the stork."* What the hell? A bird? We just wanted to know what intercourse really was and how you got pregnant from it. We should have been told that, sex is sacred and was meant to be shared only with your husband not with every boy that came knocking at your virgina *(vagina)*. We should have been told that love and intimacy were supposed to go hand in hand. If only the unspoken word had been spoken, I might have been able to avoid those dark, dingy, filthy and dangerous back allies run by doctors that butchered you in make shift offices in the middle of the night.

I didn't know that you could get pregnant the first time you had sex. At that age you are invincible. You don't think it can or will happen to you. In fact, you don't think anything can happen to you, only to someone else. My lack of knowledge kept me ignorant to the facts of life and it kept me in those make shift offices. I was rolling the dice with each abortion I had. As an adolescent the risks were high and I could have easily died.

Abortion is a topic that is very controversial. It is an issue that goes beyond political discussion. It transcends both a religious and emotionally based subject matter. You have two factions: pro-choice and pro-life. Pro-choice says "A woman has a right *(since it is her body)* to terminate a pregnancy if she wants." Whereas, pro-life says "An abortion kills a human life and can possibly do harm to a woman." What is best for a woman who is contemplating an unwanted pregnancy? Which side is right? That is a decision that has to be made by the individual woman. Our laws protect the option to terminate a pregnancy for whatever reasons. Words to the wise: Abortion should never be used as a method for birth control. That's what I was doing.

I remember one time specifically that haunts me to this day. I was in my junior year of college. It was summertime. I had planned a big 4th of July party. It was an exciting day because most of the guests in attendance were celebrating the fact they we would be college seniors in the fall. Four weeks prior to the party I discovered I was pregnant again. The panic and fear of mama came over me again so I knew what I had to do. I had to find another doctor. I felt safer subjecting myself to multiple abortions in the house of horrors than to dare tell her that I was pregnant. That would have been a fate worse than death.

There was no way I could think of having a baby in my last year of college. I had plans to travel, live the bachelorette life style and eventually attend law school. A baby was certainly not in that equation. Two days before the party I was successful in finding another doctor. You might ask "Why didn't I go back to the doctor I had before?" They weren't that easy to contact. They didn't stay in one place for too long because of the abortion laws (*it was illegal*). I found another doctor and had the procedure done and then went home. I felt a little weak but that was expected. I had lost a lot of blood this time. I figured every doctor had different methods of performing the procedure and they each had their way of getting the job done. At the time my boyfriend of two years wanted me to keep the baby and wanted for us to get married. I out voted him. I had big plans and nothing was going to stand in my way. It was my body, my life, and most importantly I would have had MY MAMA to deal with.

There was a lot of preparation to be done the day of the party. I was busy most of the day: cleaning, cooking and preparing for the evening's festivities. All of the work that was done earlier left me feeling weak and nauseated. As my guests started to arrive, I began experiencing severe stomach cramps. I didn't think much about it until the cramps were unbearable. It sent me quickly to the bathroom. I sat on the toilet bent over holding my stomach. I felt something pass through my body. I stood up to look what had dropped into the toilet. What I saw was unbelievable! It was part of the fetus or maybe the placenta I really didn't know what it was. I stood up put my hand in the toilet, pulled it out, wrapped it in some newspaper and put it under my bed. I didn't know what to do with it. I thought I would figure that out later. Somehow I was able to make it through the party. I was not really in a party mood then. All I could think about was *"What had just happened"* I knew though I needed to see a doctor. I could hardly wait until the next day to see what was wrong with me.

I went to the emergency room of the hospital the next day and signed in. When my name was called I went into the room to wait for the doctor. I was afraid to tell him about the abortion. I just told him that I was having severe stomach cramps. The doctor examined me and after the exam, he told me what was wrong. I was shocked and frightened. He explained to me that, "Whoever performed your abortion had not completed it. Your body was rejecting what was left." After that day, two pregnancies and two abortions taught me everything and anything there was to learn about birth control and that I needed to start using it. It's just too bad I had to find out the hard way. You would think I would have learned my lesson. *"A hard head makes a soft ass"* another one of Mama's sayings. My stupidity led me to go on and have yet another three pregnancies and three more abortions. What was it that I didn't get? There were no more excuses now because I knew the truth. I had been so ignorant and uniformed about sex. All of the facts about sex that my circle of friends had compiled were now null and void. Especially the one we swore by that was foolproof. We decided that, "If a boy pulled his penis out before ejaculation, there was no way you could get pregnant." I guess I proved that one wrong.

As I grew older my street smarts didn't seem to grow with me. I allowed men to feed me all the lines and flattery that they thought I wanted to hear. Like food had been for me in the past, it was a substitute and it made me feel real good. It satisfied my emotional hunger for love, even though I knew it wasn't good for me. I became their sexual hostess. Each time I ate from their plate of deception, self-hatred...became more and more of a reality for me. I was in and out of relationships. I had boyfriends like the bank had money. I looked at it like this. Men were players and I was a playa. The only difference was that I was getting played.

Graduation from college was one of the most exciting milestones in my life. I was able to get a job in my field as a Paralegal. I was hired by a top firm because I believe they needed a little *color* in the office. The pay was great so that meant it was time for me to reach the second milestone, which was moving away from home and getting my own apartment. I was only 21 years old. It was a good feeling to finally exercise my independence from my parents. I was going to be able to do what I wanted (*which obviously I was doing anyway*) and when I wanted with no repercussions. Mama was ready for me to go. I had put her thru a lot with me trying to be grown. She said, "The only way to learn about life and experience was to jump in the water and get wet." I really should not have been sent packing like that because she knew and I knew that I was not ready for the world. According to her "If you think you are grown then it's time for you to leave." Let's look at this a little closer. Mothers everywhere please "Do Not" rush your daughter(s) out of the house to live on their own if you know they are not ready socially, emotionally, especially if they lack street smarts.

What a good feeling it was to work hard all day and come home to what was yours, your space...your peace. There is one important thing that does come with independence. That's responsibility. What do I mean by that? A lot of young ladies rush to get out of the house without the maturity or understanding of what it takes to live on their own. I was ready to leave home but I was so naive to the ways of the world. I was fast especially when it came to men and dating but I was not street smart. You need a balance of the two. All the education in the world with no experience means nothing. I was in the fast lane but I didn't have a chance in hell of keeping up. I was a little fish from the pond now trying to swim in the big ocean.

I always thought I was a pretty good judge of character and always demanded respect from the men who wanted to spend their time with me. At twenty-one though, how much did I really know?

I met David riding on the city's public transportation. Oh, I forgot to tell you, not only did I leave home I left the state and moved to Washington, D.C. I traded in the country for the big city. I would see David just about everyday on my way to work so he was a familiar face. Sometimes he would drive with his compartment door open so he could watch me. He would always smile and say "*Good morning.*" We would talk about work and other topics in between the stops. He was always pleasant and spoke to me with respect. I really liked how he presented himself to me. As time progressed, David asked me for my telephone number. I did not hesitate to give it to him. We spoke on the telephone for several weeks before he asked me out on a date. I felt very comfortable with him and (*like I said I thought I was a good judge of character*) so I figured why not. That was a bad move.

We decided that Saturday would be a good night for our first date. I had no idea that this would be our first and last date. He suggested we go out to dinner and go to a movie. David was going to pick me up at 6pm. He assured me that we were going to have a fun evening. I was really looking forward to spending time with him and (*not just on the train*) because he seemed like a nice guy.

The doorbell rang and I was impressed that he was on time. When I opened the door, he was well dressed (*There's nothing like a well dressed man who looks good and smells good.*) with a picture perfect smile. He presented me with a dozen roses, which I took and placed inside a vase before we left. He was quite the gentleman, opening my car door and helping me inside. Of course, every lady should be treated that way and we should not accept anything less. He started the car and then David informed me that he had left his credit card at his apartment. It was only going to take a few minutes for him to grab it and then we would be on our way.

When we got there, he invited me to go in with him because he didn't want to leave me alone in the car. I didn't see any harm in that because we were only going to be there a minute. He parked in the alley and we walked up the stairs to his back door. He told me to "Have a seat while he grabbed the credit card." A few minutes passed and David returned from his bedroom. I thought we were ready to go. I was sadly mistaken. He did not have the credit card but he did have a gun that was pointed directly at me.

He ordered me to *"Get on the sofa,* then he blindfolded me. Before I could resist, he threw me down and began tearing off my clothes. Everything was happening so fast. I couldn't think straight. Certainly, thoughts to scream came to mind but they were soon dismissed. David must have read my mind because he told me "You had better not think of screaming or making any loud noises." I even thought about running for the door but it had several locks on it. I knew if or *when* David pulled the trigger on the gun, the bullet would be faster than me. He was in total control and he backed it up with that hard cold steel against my temple. I heard him cock the gun so I knew then that he meant business.

In this life you always have choices. I didn't have to take it. I could have fought back or screamed but my choice was neither of these. I knew if I had chosen any of them or made any wrong move, David would have put me six feet under. I asked him "Why are you doing this to me?" He just told me "Shut up!" With that revolver to my head I couldn't see that I had much choice. I suffered in silence and completely surrendered.

I laid there asking God to "Please allow me to walk away from this nightmare alive." I was assaulted numerous times and somehow he managed to never let go of that gun to my head. I looked into his eyes with horror and in my twenty-one years on this earth I suddenly knew and understood for the first time the meaning of fear. I've heard people say, "They can smell and taste the scent of fear." They were right. It made me sick to my stomach. I had no idea how long I was there. Time seemed to stand still. I was held prisoner for what seemed like an eternity. I became invisible to myself and was void of any feeling.

On that third warm Saturday night in September, God clearly answered two of my prayers. The first one was "I was able to walk away with my life." I'll tell you the second one later. David ordered me to "Get up! Put your clothes on!" I tried to get dressed quickly but his patience was short. He barely gave me a chance to put them on. Before I knew it, he grabbed me. I was half dressed, in only my torn skirt and blouse. My bra, panties and shoes were left behind. He taped my mouth before we left with duct tape. He grabbed my arm and we exited out the back door and down the stairs to his car. I wanted to run screaming down the alley but I decided that would have not done any good. I would have been shot down like an animal or beat like a punching bag and besides my mouth was taped shut. Who would hear muffling noises? David shoved me into the car, put the blindfold back on my face and drove off. I didn't know if I was going to live or die. His next words to me were "Get out the car bitch!" He snatched the blindfold off my face and leaned over to open the door. He pushed me out and sped away. I was bruised scratched, half naked, and traumatized, but I was alive and home!

I remained on the ground where I landed momentarily crying through the duct tape that was still on my mouth. I was hoping that I could make sense out of what had just happened to me. I tried to figure out what I could have possibly done to deserve this. I realized it was a hopeless feat. I got up, pulled the duct tape away from my mouth, hurried into my apartment and bolted the door. I think this is where the real nightmare began because I was alone now with the (date from hell) playing over and over in my head.

I called a girlfriend and told her what happened. In fact she was the only one who knew for years. She came over immediately and told me "You have to go to the emergency room to get checked out and make a report with the police." I chose neither. I decided that I didn't want to be examined. I wasn't going to put myself through a thousand questions from doctors or policemen as if I was the one that did something wrong. I was not emotionally able to withstand that. I did contemplate over and over "If I had made the right decision? Should I have turned him in?" I didn't know where he lived because we parked in the alley so there were no addresses to remember. I couldn't identify the building but I did know where he worked. I guess I was too scared. I feared for my life. He knew where I lived and where I worked. How did I know if he would actually get locked up and for how long? Would I have to testify in court? Would the attorneys shred my character and make me look like the criminal? I preferred to live the rest of my life with those unanswered questions. I do live with the guilt that I could have possibly kept him from doing this to someone else because I'm sure he did.

I just wanted this whole thing to be over. I never wanted to see his face again. By the way the second part of my prayer was answered, "I didn't get pregnant and I didn't contract any sexually transmitted diseases." AMEN

### The Topic Of Date Rape is Marked Urgent!!!

What is the first comment most people say when they hear someone has been raped? *"They must have been dressed too provocative"* or *"They must have done something to encourage it."* This is so stereotypical of some people.

When you are forced to have sex without consent while you are on a date, it's known as DATE RAPE or ACQUAINTANCE RAPE.

- ➢ It should be understood that rape has nothing to do with love or passion.
- ➢ Rape is an act of aggression and violence. It is forced sex against someone's will. It is unfair for people to point

fingers and say, "They were "asking for it." Really? Who asks to be raped?

➤ The person who is raped is NEVER to blame. It is always the rapist's fault.

When you are dating someone, respect is the key to having a healthy relationship. If a person really cares about you, s/he will not force or pressure you to have sex. Fortunately, I was not given any drugs to dull my senses. Generally, alcohol and date rape drugs like rohypnol, gamma-hydroxybutyrae, or ketamine can be easily mixed into many beverages/drinks. It can cloud your thinking and cause you to become unconscious and blackout so you are unaware of what happened or what took place. When you are out on a date and you choose to have a drink...

➤ Watch how your drink is being prepared.
➤ Drugs can be slipped into your drink at a party or a bar without your knowledge.
➤ Never drink from your cup/glass if you leave it unattended. If you return to your unattended drink, avoid drinking it. Obtain a fresh drink.

Date rape can happen to anyone even when precautions are taken. It can be very difficult to think or talk about the incident. Don't make the same mistake I did. Thinking it could be brushed under the rug. GET HELP!

➤ If you've been physically injured, go to a hospital's emergency room immediately. Contact a friend, family member, or someone you feel comfortable telling what happened.
➤ If you choose to report the rape, contact the police immediately. Do not change clothes or wash your body.
➤ For immediate emotional support call a rape crisis center hotline.

There were a lot of questions running through my mind. I wasn't sure what to do. I opted to do nothing. Being raped by someone you know is not only physically damaging but also emotionally traumatic. If you can at some point seek crisis counseling or a mental health professional to begin the healing process, do it.

I always thought I was strong, independent and could get through anything. As the weeks went by I soon realized that I was vulnerable just like everyone else. No matter how hard I tried, the nightmare continued to follow me. Months later I started experiencing symptoms of severe nervousness. I actually thought, *"I was going crazy."* I didn't know what was happening to me. I did know whatever was happening to me, I would not have wished it on my worst enemy. The nervousness and nightmares were so unbearable. I finally sought professional help. After an extensive medical interview and physical examination I was diagnosed with generalized anxiety. This is a mood disorder characterized by continuous and or nonspecific worries that promote a presence or feeling of danger. The doctor informed me that generalized anxiety is very common and actually affects millions of people.

Thanks to the date from hell, panic attacks were the result of my anxiety. Many times I thought I was having a heart attack. My heart was pounding so fast, my pulse was rapid, I was cold, I couldn't breathe, and I couldn't eat or sleep. I thought I was going to die. I was having these attacks so often that I was prescribed a psychotropic drug to calm me down (*paxil*). Instead, it intensified my symptoms and I became worse than ever before. I felt like I was literally coming out of my body. You really have to be careful with those drugs because the side effects can be devastating. They can make your symptoms worse. I didn't waste any time flushing those pills down the toilet. I told the doctor how they had affected me and he said we could try a *different* prescription. I thought *we*? He wasn't taking anything or experiencing all the side effects. I told him I wasn't taking any more of those pills! He suggested that I make an appointment with a clinical counselor for help. I was on my third clinical counselor when I realized these therapy sessions were not working for me. That's when I decided to see if I had any medical skills of my own. I started researching natural herbs for anxiety and found several that were beneficial for me. I began taking them on a regular basis. Eventually the symptoms subsided and the panic attacks have pretty much become a thing of the past. If I get too stressed out I may have an attack but it is controllable now.

The past still seems to haunt me from time to time. As the years go by, I realize that I have not totally healed from this incident. The trauma lingers and I can see how it has affected my life in many ways, especially my relationships with men (*I don't give them a pass on anything*) In other words I don't take no shit off of them (*of course we're not supposed to anyway*).

At times I have bouts with claustrophobia. It is very difficult for me to stay for long periods of time in enclosed small spaces. The psychologist explained to me that it is the result of being held down and confined by my rapist in a small space. He was covering me with his body and I could not move (*which makes a lot of sense*). I wonder at some point will I ever get healed and bury this disturbing incident forever. I don't know. For now I do no that I am a survivor and...

**I thank God EVERYDAY for that!**

*ten*

# Murder on My Mind

"I hid the kitchen knife in my book bag and
left for school. It was my only hope. I would
use it if I had to. If Amy messed with me
today, I knew I was going to kill her...then
my problems would be over. Enough was
enough. I wasn't going to take it anymore."

*DeAnn Cambridge, 11 years young, Atlanta, Georgia*

My name is DeAnn. I don't have a daughter but one day I might.
I'm only eleven years old but I wanted to tell my story too in hopes
that girl's my age and even boys will learn from my story. I'm sure
what I have to say will help and be a lesson to everyone. I've heard
my problem talked about at school, church, on television, in news-
papers, magazines, and even on the radio. I was told, *"It has always
been a problem."* It seems to be happening more and more. It happens to adults just as much but in my case especially to children.
My story takes place at the school I attended and at other schools
all across the Nation. I didn't know that there could be so much
pressure for an eleven year old. This is supposed to be a fun time for
a kid my age. Instead, I was suffering and very unhappy. My relatives, teachers and friends have always labeled me as a shy girl. I am

a little quiet and I don't talk a whole lot but what happened to me turned me into a different person.

My grandmother used to tell me, "Sticks and stones may break your bones but words will never hurt you." Well, that's not true. Words do hurt. Words will make you cry. My mom used to say that, "Kids will be kids. Boys will be boys". They tend to boss each other around and sometimes they get into pushing matches." She also said, "In my day they used to call it picking on you." "*Today it is called bullying*." Bullies can be boys, girls and even adults.

### Here are the facts.

➤ They look for your weakness. They smell your fear. Bullies make you feel bad on purpose and they're really good at it. How do they do this? By name calling, hitting, pushing, kicking, peer pressure and even spreading rumors about you.

➤ Bullies don't care who they hurt or how they hurt their victims. Who do bullies pick on? Those who are smaller than they are. Those who they think won't stand up to them. Those who don't have a lot of friends that will help them stand up to a bully.

➤ What are some of the reasons bullies behave the way they do? They want to look big and important to their friends. It makes them feel better about themselves. They enjoy feeling powerful over others.

➤ Bullies are sometimes bullied by someone else. You may not have thought about it but beatings, slapping, hitting, pushing, shouting and name calling by your parents makes them bullies too.

Maybe this is where all my problems began. Parents are supposed to be the ones who protect and take care of their kids from being hurt. It's possible that parents who act like bullies were also bullied as children or even as adults on their jobs. Bullies like to be in control. Since kids are smaller which makes them easy targets to push around.

I have witnessed and experienced bullying from my parents and my friends parents. When I visit my friends house Trina, I can see how bullying affects her. If she doesn't respond immediately to her father when he calls her, he will yell at her and tell her "Go to your room! No dinner for you!" Most times when I am over there he will say mean things to her. He tells her, "No one wants to be your friend. They just feel sorry for you. That's why they hang around you." When I get home from her house, I will usually call to see if she is okay but her father will not let me talk to her. He will curse at me and hang up the phone.

I remember another time we were eating some cookies and drinking milk at her kitchen table. She accidentally knocked her glass over. Her father yelled at her "You are too old to be so clumsy. Now clean up the mess you made." He threw a towel at her and said, "Hurry and clean it up!" As she was cleaning up the spilled milk, her father taunted her saying "You are as slow as a turtle." All I could see was that he was a big bully. I understand that parents are under a lot of pressure. They are dealing with work, paying bills and taking care of other responsibilities but that is no reason to lash out at their child and bully them. I'm sure it's not easy being an adult but it isn't easy being a child either.

The effects of bullying can be physical, emotional, and mental. Sometimes it can affect how you think. Physically, a child can come home from school with cuts, bruises, and scratches. Emotionally, kids can become nervous or jittery and suffer from low self-esteem. They may also be sad and have different moods at school and/or at home. Bullying can affect a kid's thinking. They can lose interest in school or become unable to think clearly. A child may even take a different route home that may take longer or travel through a dangerous neighborhood just to avoid a bully when walking to or from school. Some kids just think missing school and staying home will make the problem go away.

My mother has two daughters. I am the oldest. I believe she has always favored my younger sister over me. Why do I say that? I'm the one that's always getting yelled at and mistreated. I try to do the things my mom wants me to do but I never seem to please her. When she yells at me I cry. When I cry I can't seem to stop. The more my mom yells at me the more I cry. She gets so angry with me and slaps me across my face so hard that I fly across the room like a rag doll. After she does this, I feel so weak, helpless, and afraid. She doesn't care where she is or who is around, when she bullies me. She will act like this in front of friends, relatives and even people she doesn't know.

I remember one time we were in a store shopping and the cart I was pushing accidentally hit the back of her heel. She started yelling at me and I told her I was sorry. She turned around and started yelling at me. You already know what I did. I started crying. She yelled at me even more "You are so stupid for always crying." There were customers who were standing nearby shopping and saw what was going on. They came up to her and told her "If you don't stop yelling at your child, we will call the police and have you arrested." She didn't care. She told them "Y'all need to mind your own business and leave me the fuck alone." The store manager came and told her "You have to leave the store now!" She dragged me out the store by my arm.

Don't get me wrong. I know my mother loves me because she takes good care of me. She doesn't neglect me. She is a good provider and makes sure that I'm involved in activities that I like to do for fun after school. I don't know why she treats me like she does. I suspect and was told that maybe she was bullied as a child, maybe as a wife, or maybe even by her boss at work. The point I want to make is how I became a victim of bullying and finally a bully myself.

One day, in social studies class we were learning about suicide bombers. Some of them were children who kill themselves because of their beliefs. I began thinking about children right here in the United States of America who commit suicide for various different reasons. They kill themselves because they have been teased or bullied because they are gay, too fat too skinny, laughed at or talked about because of a physical or mental challenge, or they don't wear all of the latest clothes like the other kids.

I have read and heard many stories about children who have hung themselves in their bedrooms with belts, cords or sheets. There are so many stories of kids who have been beaten up, lost an eye or hearing, and have been permanently scarred physically for life. Young people my age turn to suicide because they are too young to deal with their emotions. When you're feeling sad, alone, angry or frustrated, suicide may be your only choice for handling these feelings. In our class we were also talking about terrorism in our country and how we are fighting to keep *"The United States"* and its citizens safe. Well, What about the terrorist in the classroom? I'm talking about the bullies. We should do something about that to keep kids in our schools safe and on the streets.

A childhood friend of mine committed suicide when she was twelve years old. Chloe lived on the 3rd floor of our apartment complex. We were really good friends. We hung out together almost every day and every weekend. Chloe used to tell me all the time how the kids at her school would tease her because she didn't wear all the latest clothes like the rest of her classmates. Her mother was a single parent like mine. She wasn't able to afford all the things she wanted because she had to use her money to take care of her brother who was having trouble with his vision. He was hit in the eye while playing baseball. Now, he has difficulty with his vision. She had to pay for his medical visits to the doctor.

Chloe used to come home always feeling sad. I tried to cheer her up but it didn't seem to do any good. She said, "The kids call me raggedy and say I'm not cool. They laugh at me. They point at me and throw food at me during lunchtime when I'm in the cafeteria." It seems as we get older how we look becomes very important. Everybody wants to fit in and be accepted as part of the crowd. It's really too bad that material things are way more important than who we are as a person.

One day Chloe was on her way home and some of the kids at school were following her. They surrounded her and started pulling her hair." She showed me the spots where her hair came out. I asked her was she going to tell her mother? She said, "I don't want to be a snitch and get them in trouble." She felt that the other kids would start bothering her too if she told. I told my mom about how they were teasing Chloe and bullying her at school. She said that she would talk to Chloe's Mom about it but my mom never got around to it. Two days later Chloe went into the bathroom and never came out. Her brother found her. She had filled the bathtub with water, swallowed some aspirins, went into a coma and drowned in the bathtub. Her brother called his mother who was still at work and told her the news. It was hard to believe that my best friend was dead all because she didn't wear designer clothes. I felt my mom could have done something to prevent Chloe from committing suicide since I had told her what was going on but she never got around to it. Like I said, I'm shy and pretty quiet at school and at home, but that would soon change.

It started when Amy came to my school as a new student. She was much bigger than most of the other kids in the class and was not very friendly but for some reason she seemed to like me and wanted to be my friend but that was not her plan at all. I was smart in school and studied hard to get good grades. I would always help out in the classroom when my teachers asked me. Amy did not like this because she was the new girl and wanted the attention that I was getting. She started to call me names "teacher's pet, nerd, bookworm." Physically, I was much smaller and shorter than Amy and if you want to know the truth, I was afraid of her.

I was powerless when she was around. Her cruel words and actions made me very sad. It made me think of how Chloe must have felt. It wasn't fun anymore coming to school. I hated it. Amy started making me do things I didn't want to and if I didn't do them she would threaten to beat me up. She was either teasing me or pushing me around. When I tried to tell her that I didn't want to get in trouble, she would call me "*Stupid*" and tell me "*that I was a pussy.*" Soon I stopped listening in class, I was no longer paying attention to the teacher or doing my work. I was too busy thinking about what Amy was going to make me do next. My classmates wouldn't or couldn't help me because they were afraid of Amy and they didn't want to get beat up by her. My classmates kept quiet and tried to mind their own business. They knew that she was threatening and bullying me but they felt there was nothing they could do.

I had been a student with perfect behavior and good grades. Now, I was like Amy. Her negative influence and bossiness led me to pushing other girls around and fighting. It's funny because in a way by me being so shy, I started feeling like I was powerful and in control of other people and it felt kind of good. During my lunchtime I would try to hide from her but she would always find me and demand that I sit at her table and eat lunch with her. Amy would make me talk about and make fun of other kids. Not only was I fighting and making others feel bad now but she also had me stealing money out of my classmates' book bags and giving it to her.

I was miserable, scared, and alone and had no one to turn to for help. My grades started dropping. I wasn't doing well on my tests or assignments. I started having stomachaches, headaches, crying spells, trouble sleeping and as much as I loved to eat, I had lost my appetite. All of these (*I was told later*) are a result of bullying. One of the girls in my class was quiet like I was and never bothered anyone. Well, Amy told me "If you don't fight her, I'm going to tell the teacher that you are the one stealing money out of the book bags." I knew I would be in worse trouble for stealing than for fighting as if one could be worse than the other. I didn't have much choice so I went over to her, pushed her out of her seat and started punching her. My teacher, Ms. Adams, called security and they both took me to the principal's office. They called my mother to come and get me. My mom had to leave work early and I was suspended for five days so she was really mad at me. I paid for it when I got home.

My behavior at school made its way to my house. I started bullying my sister Gail. I would tease her and call her names (*because she had a stuttering problem*) and that would make her cry. When Gail told our mom what I said to her I would beat her up. Since she always got all the attention from my mother, I didn't feel bad. If she had any snacks because she was always buying cookies and chips, I would take them from her and she would tell on me again. That meant more trouble for me. My mother started calling me names. Mom said, "You are a bad seed." Anytime I would come near my mom, she would push me out of her way. I was like the cream in a sandwich cookie. I was being bullied on both sides, at home and at school. None of my family could figure out why I was acting like this. My teachers couldn't figure it out either. No one had a clue that I was a victim of bullying at school and at home.

I kept getting suspended for fighting and my grades continued to drop. I didn't see how things were going to get any better with Amy always on my back. I kept asking myself "Why couldn't my teachers see what was going on?" I wasn't doing these things because I wanted to. Couldn't they see how Amy was bossing me around and making me do all these bad things? Why didn't I just ask for help? The answer to this question is not an easy one. I felt helpless and scared. I thought I would be able to handle all of this on my own. I kept thinking, "This won't last long. It will go away". I wondered would my teachers believe me or understand what was going on if I told them what was happening to me. One thing I did learn from Amy was that if you act scared and cry the bully has accomplished what they set out to do, to be mean and hurtful. Now, the person who has expressed those negativities has the power and control over you. In most cases bullies can make you do things that you don't want to. This is where Amy got me.

Teachers are so busy that sometimes they cannot see everything going on in and out of the classroom. I felt I was trapped because I couldn't tell my teachers what Amy was making me do. I didn't want to tell my mother because she didn't even do anything to help my friend Chloe. She probably would have laughed and made fun of me for not standing up for myself and fighting Amy (*I don't think a parent should ever encourage their child to fight*) there has to be another way.

I woke up one day and decided I wasn't going to take this crap from Amy anymore. I got dressed for school and then I went to the kitchen. I took a knife out the drawer, put it in my book bag, and left for school. It was my only hope. If Amy bothered me today, I was going to kill her and then my problems would all be over. Enough was enough. I wasn't going to take this anymore.

For some reason I felt really strong. Today, I wasn't scared of Amy. When I arrived at school she was waiting for me on the school playground. She motioned me to come over. She was ready to give me my assignment for the day. I don't know where the words came from but they came out of my mouth. I looked her in the eye and told her "I am not going to do your dirty work anymore." The next thing I knew she pushed me so hard I almost fell backward. It would have been better for her if I had because I wouldn't have been able to get to my book bag. I quickly opened the zipper of my bag and pulled the knife out. Just as I was about to stab Amy a hand came from out of nowhere and grabbed my hand. It was the school security personnel, Mr. Thomas. He saw Amy push me and he could tell I was angry after that. He saw me pull the knife out of my book bag. It's a good thing he was there or I might be locked up now for murder. Mr. Thomas took Amy and me to the office and our parents were called to meet with the principal.

Amy's mother pressed charges against me. The police were called and a report was made. Lucky for me I wasn't taken to jail. I was released to the custody of my mother until my court date. She was crying so hard. I felt really bad because I never wanted to hurt my mom. Mr. Carson, the principal wanted to know what happened on the playground and why I brought a knife to school. I told him, "Amy had been bullying me for several months. I was scared to say anything because she threatened to beat me up if I did." Her mother immediately called me a liar!" My mom stepped in to defend me and the yelling match between them began. Mr. Carson had to calm Amy's mom and my mom down. I continued to explain that, "Amy was always pushing me around and telling me what to do." I told them about the money she made me steal from the book bags and how she made me fight other girls. Of course Amy denied everything I said. Amy said, "You were the one who was starting all the trouble." After I shared with Mr. Carson what all she made me do and everything she did to me, Amy got mad and tried to fight me right in the office. Mr. Carson had to pull her away from me.

One of my teachers, Ms. Mason, was there and spoke on my behalf. She said, "Before Amy transferred to our school, DeAnn was a model student. She was a quiet girl and never bothered anyone. She always did her work and received good grades. I knew something was wrong but I didn't know exactly what it was." Several girls from my class were called into the office for questioning. When they arrived, you could tell they were afraid to say anything. Angie was the first one to speak. She was tired of being afraid of Amy. She told Mr. Carson "I saw Amy push DeAnn around and heard her say, "If you tell anything to anyone or don't do what I tell you I'll beat you up." The others spoke up as well and told what they had seen and heard. Mr. Carson asked them "Why didn't you speak up before now." They explained, "We were scared that Amy might beat us up or make us do bad things too."

Next, Mr. Carson called the school counselor, Ms. Jennings into his office and asked her to bring Amy's file with information from her other school to him. In the meantime Amy's mother kept yelling and swearing at Mr. Carson saying, "This matter is not about my daughter it's about hers (*pointing to my mother*)." My Mom stood up and I thought she was going to hit Amy's mom dead in the mouth. My mom yelled, "Be quiet! There are kids in this office!" Amy's mom continued to yell and call everybody "liars"!

Ms. Jennings returned to the office with the file. It seemed Amy had a record of bullying kids at four other schools she had previously attended. It stated that she had been dealing with behavioral problems since the third grade. She was suspended from school numerous times for fighting and stealing. Instead of Amy getting herself in trouble she was going to find someone else to do her dirty work this time and that person was me. The meeting finally ended. Amy's mother said, "I don't care what you all say I'll get my justice in court!"

When my Mom and I got home, she had a long talk with me. She explained to me that her mom and grandmother had both bullied her while she was growing up. They called me names and pushed me around just like I have been doing to you. I am responsible for what has happened to you. I allowed that bullying to continue. I'm repeating history." Mom called it *"learned behavior."* Learned behavior means if somebody does something to you enough times, more than likely you may do it to someone else. That's exactly what happened. She apologized and asked for my forgiveness. She said, "I'll never bully you again." I had suffered many years of her mistreating me. I didn't know if I could believe her or not. Only time would tell.

My court day came quickly. I was nervous. No, I was scared because I didn't know what was going to happen. I had never been in trouble before let alone been in a courtroom. We went in and took a seat up front. My case was the second one called. We approached the bench with our lawyer. Judge Kramer read my file and asked me if I understood the seriousness of my actions (*attempted murder with a deadly weapon*). She talked to me about the student code of conduct from my school district and said that they have the authority to expel or otherwise discipline any student found to have a knife or weapon on school property.

I was asked to explain "Why I brought a knife to school?" I began to tell her my story of being bullied and the things that were done to me at school and at home. I told the judge "I was tired of being picked on. Amy had pushed me to my limit and I guess I kinda lost it. That's why I brought the knife to school to protect myself." Judge Kramer listened carefully to my story and what I had to say. She said, "It was bad enough you brought a knife to school but taking the knife out of your book bag was intent to do bodily harm. Since you did not carry out the act of inflicting harm this would be considered in her decision. She indicated that I did not have a previous conviction of possessing a weapon on school property and no other prior offenses. Judge Kramer looked at my school file and stated that, "I was a good student prior to this incident according to written statements from your teachers". Mr. Carson and Ms. Jennings were willing to speak so highly on your behalf. It's going to be my decision to dismiss this case with six months probation. There was another stipulation. The judge sternly expressed "If you ever return to my court again I will send you to a juvenile detention facility." Mr. Carson did not expel me from school but I was suspended from school for ten days. I did learn one important thing from this experience. Whenever you're having a problem, don't try to handle it yourself. Always, find an adult you can go to and ask for help.

Bullying is a threat to students' physical, mental and emotional safety at school, home or anywhere. It can definitely impact negatively on your ability to learn and socialize in this society. Bullying has been extended thanks to the wonderful world of technology. It has created a new way kids can verbally abuse each other. It is called "cyber bullying." The media outlets have utilized various devices and equipment such as cell phones, texting, internet, social media (*YouTube, Facebook, Twitter, Instagram*) These outlets were

supposed to be used for positive activities, entertainment and inter-
action to connect kids and adults with their friends and family.
Some are using it as a tool to send hurtful and damaging messages
that can:

> Be used 24 hours a day/7 days a week
> Messages can be left anonymously protecting the sender's
  identity.

Bullying of any kind is mean and cruel. It doesn't matter how or
why it is done.

Teachers and staff should pay close attention to what's happening inside and outside of their classrooms, at home and in the community. If a child starts acting out and it's not their usual behavior,
don't just ignore it. Find out what is going on with the child. Do
some questioning and make some observations.

### Parents Teachers and Administrators Be Aware and Care

> Target places where bullying might take place. Check
  bathrooms, playground, hallways, buses, cellphones and
  computers.
> Let students know that telling is not snitching (You are pro-
  tecting and keeping someone safe and from possible harm.).
> Record incidents and investigate them.
> If you see it, intervene.
> Let students know that bullying is not acceptable. There
  will be consequences for this behavior.
> Teach and encourage positive behavior.
> Teach skills on how to handle bullying when it occurs.

Oh, I forgot there is one more important thing that I wanted to
say about bullying in the media, specifically television. Producers,
directors, writers, actors, actresses should stop the bullying and
violence viewed on their television shows, movies, programs and

reality shows. We know they only care about who's watching and what the ratings are. Somebody has to be responsible and think about the messages that are being portrayed. Cursing, fighting, name calling and chasing someone across the room to slap them is not what real women do. Producers, directors, writers, actors and actresses will draw the viewers in with all this drama that they think is very entertaining and exciting. Sure, we don't have to look at or watch them (*nobody's making us*).

It is up to our parents to teach us what is and is not appropriate behavior and what programs are acceptable for viewing. Images are very important to young girls in this society. A lot of us will act out what we see. As we are growing up we need positive nourishment. We are looking toward adults to feed us responsibly. You should remember that we are the future women of the world. Give us some role models that we can identify with and look up to. Ask yourself if you want your daughters or other young girls growing up to be the next reality star,

**Or, maybe even the next bully?**

# Epilogue

## "Be yourself. Everyone else is taken."

## Oscar Wilde

The narratives you have just read are stories that could character-ize a culture of women from anywhere in the world. As women we have all experienced some trials and tribulations in our lives. Some were positive, others were challenging. Many of their issues that were expressed have been our issues too. For some of us they still are! These women wanted to disclose some of the teachings that they felt were lacking in the process of growing up with their moth-ers. It is not to say that if their mothers had prepared them with these lessons that their lives would have turned out any better or differently.

This book was not written for the purpose of playing the *"blame game."* It was not intended to point fingers toward single, married, working, or stay at home moms or the men that have passed through their lives. It was written to encourage an open dialogue to stimu-late more communication, resolve and address relevant concerns and issues for women and children.

We must get past the days where inquisitive little girls ques-tions were met with one-word answers or no answers at all. As mothers, we do not know everything. We don't have all the answers. I've heard many times that *"the best way to learn something is to teach it to someone else."* As a global community we are connected now more than ever with technology, enabling us to hear the many voices of other women who have walked the walk and want to share their life experiences freely. This is powerful! The road of life will never be smooth and there is no magic charm that will protect our children or protect us from all the bumps and rough spots in the road. We can affirm that the more information we do provide will make the journey a little less tumultuous.

The overarching themes of body image, self-esteem, education, financial responsibilities, relationships, substance abuse and other pertinent topics for women and young girls directly and indirectly affect us all. They are intensified and magnified more today than ever before, especially for our teenage girls. These same issues have plagued our generations and they will continue for years to come.

As we look forward to the future to overcome these ever-present obstacles we must remember that the home is a child's first school and classroom. This is where life's lessons begin to formulate and the foundation is laid. The mother is the first teacher, role model and influence in a child's life. When there is an atmosphere of open communication in the home it begins to create a mutual trust between the mother and the daughter. The child learns to trust the reliability of the mother's teachings. However, a mother can only teach what she knows, whether it is good or bad.

The first five or six years of a child's life are critical in the development of becoming a secure, emotionally independent adult. Principles that teach acceptance, respect of authority, self-discipline, a basic knowledge of health, nutrition, physiology, self-worth and idealism rather than materialism will set the tone of how the child will develop and what their expectations of self and others will be.

When we take on the role of motherhood, there is no introduction. It is given to us instantly without any preparation. We do not have the opportunity to ease into it or test the waters. We have to be ready. It has already been established that teaching and parenting skills have not been perfected or patented, but we have to start somewhere.

### Start Talking To Your Daughters Early

Let's not wait until they are twenty-one years old to begin discussing important topics. Begin the conversation while they are young and continue to repeat the discussions about life and its aspects. Teach them to love the skin they're in. We currently live in an image conscientious world where too much emphasis has been placed on physical beauty in our society. We are currently in a place where our young girls have become commodities. Their breast size and buttocks, designer bags, good hair, and tiny dress sizes have become the standard to measure their status, worth, value and popularity. We have become reality show zombies tuning into shows that depict women as crazed, insecure females, chasing after men, cheating, lying, seeking glitz, glamour, and fame as well as fighting and scratching to get to the top of an unrealistic fantasy world.

It is important for young women to feel good about the way they are and not depend on a man or anything superficial to define who they are. Now, that's a real reality show! It's a travesty that women have now chosen to be pretty and charming and sell themselves as objects to a man or men with the highest income or most expensive car. We have more to offer than an outer appearance. We deserve more than volatile dysfunctional relationships and a life of drama and self-exploitation. As women, we have a moral obligation and duty to our future generations to acknowledge and recognize the incredible strides women have made throughout North America and the entire world. We must break the myths and stereotypes that are currently portrayed in society's mentality, the media and other social networks.

We do not have to romance and whore our way to the top for a ticket to success. We are quite capable of aspiring to be entrepreneurs, heads of corporate businesses, breaking that glass ceiling... or whatever our career goals we have chosen to fulfill. We can even fill the position of super woman if we want to. We should continue to set our goals high, focus and break through societal norms and views that continue to shackle and define who we are as women.

Self-esteem is the glue that holds your thoughts and feelings about yourself together. These thoughts and feelings can be negative or positive. You can't buy self-esteem. It is generally influenced by the relationships and experiences that begin first in the home. The negative side of self-esteem can create an unhappy personal life. You are inclined to have minimal self-confidence and will exhibit poor work ethics and or school performance. A distorted view of self and others can become a reality. On the positive side, you are able to accept challenges, build and maintain a level of self-confidence and can express yourself in a confident manner. You are free to declare who you are without reservations and inhibitions.

If you want to improve your self-esteem, start by being a friend to yourself. Take the time to identify and accept your strengths. You would be surprised at how many you have. Try to work on your weaknesses and personality flaws. If you don't know what they are, ask someone and I bet they will be more than happy to tell you. Don't be so hard on yourself. Give yourself a pat on the back daily for encouragement and praise. If you don't love yourself, who will? We all need alone time in our own space to think things through and to participate in activities that you enjoy.

All of us need verbal praise, rewards and approval when a job has been well done. When we give compliments rather than criticism this helps to further build self-esteem. Personally, identify the things that make you feel good about yourself. Focus and appreciate the things you do have rather than the things you don't. Surround yourself with friends that encourage the things you are trying to accomplish. Positive people will bring positive vibrations. Negative people can only bring negativity. They are toxic and will poison and kill your spirit. Avoid and drop these people like your life depends on it.

I don't think there is a woman on the face of this earth that does not at some point in time compare herself to another woman. Avoid comparing your self to others. Unfortunately, society has instilled in us to *"compete" or "Look out for #1."* When we see what others have, we think that we must have that as well. That's not true. We have to decide. "What we do want?" and "Do we want or need it?" Let's start with appreciating the gifts and strengths we do have. Whether you believe it or not, there is something you have that someone else is admiring and wishing s/he had.

### Are You A Parent Or A Friend?

Guidance is more important than being your daughters BFF *best friend forever.* It is important to determine where and how you will draw the line between being a friend and being a parent to your child. Children need structure and discipline. Our hopes are that in the end they will thank you for it just like we are thanking those mothers who were able to, *"put their foot down"* right where it belonged.

### The Key to Communication is to Keep an Open Mind

Be open and honest when you talk with your daughter(s). Children especially teens are more willing to share their thoughts and feelings when you are nonjudgmental. They will close the door on you and shut down if you approach or respond to them in an accusatory, angry or authoritarian tone. You always want your daughter(s) to feel safe, valued, respected and secure. Tell them, "I am human. I make mistakes. I have faced some of the same issues, problems and challenges that you are facing." It's all right to share with them. Be careful though, how much of your personal experiences you discuss. You may not want your daughter(s) to know that you had sex at thirteen years old or smoked marijuana in high school. This kind of information can come back and haunt you. Telling her *"Do as I say and not as I do"* will not go very far with her. The first thing that she will say to you is "You did it and you turned out ok, so why can't I?"

Setting healthy boundaries can be confusing. It is hard to determine how strict or permissive you should be. Each situation will be different. You want to promote a sense of responsibility without pushing or triggering any rebellious behavior. Don't wait until they are older to set limits. Start early. Be specific about what the consequences will be if they dishonor the house rules and then enforce them.

### Get Organized And Start Making Life Decisions

Blueprints, goals, ambitions, mission, intentions or whatever you want to call them create a purpose for your life. Unfortunately, we cannot keep a child in the house until they reach adulthood to protect them. Mistakes will be made. That is how we learn. In doing so we can pass it on and share with others our successes and tribulations.

As mothers we must provide the necessary tools as they travel on the highway of life. You would not go on a road trip without knowing where you are going or how to get there. Most likely you would consult and rely on sources that would direct you in order to arrive there safely and in a timely manner. It is the same as planning your future. Now, you may veer from the road and hit a few bumps from time to time along the way. You may even lose track of where you are heading. However, with guidance and support you can and will reach your final destination.

It's a whole new age and time from the days I knew as a little girl growing up. Certainly, we have our challenges as does every generation. As women, we continue to stand strong. We are still the fabric and foundation of the family. We are the link that bridges the past to the future. We can draw from our past experiences and the lessons learned to begin sharing this knowledge that will enlighten and empower our young women.

We can't shield or protect our daughters every step of the way but we can support them as best we can. It is our responsbility to instill in our young women who they are. Inform them that they always have control of the wheel. They have the power to steer their life in the direction they want to go. They can accept or reject surrounding influences or pick those that inspire and motivate them. If you want to succeed, there is a powerful force within. When acknowledged you can and will accomplish anything. As we move forward toward the future, keep in mind that our daughters will soon take the lead.

**Our time has come to pass the torch!!!**

CPSIA information can be obtained
at www.ICGtesting.com
Printed in the USA
FSOW01n0508040717
35954FS